Not More of the Same

For Coral and Michael Pavitt -

who helped to shape what is to be

found herein.

With appreciation and love,

Not More of the Same

Lewis Watling

Lewis Watling

Given to Rorma

2015

Not More of the Same

Published by Lewis Watling
© Lewis Watling 2008

ISBN: 978-0-620-41626-9
Cover and interior designed and produced by Mousehand:
www.mousehand.co.za
Set in Adobe Garamond Pro

Contents

IV CHILDREN OF TRANSITION

V POEMS OF TRANSITION

XI A SPIRAL OF ALTERED REPETITIONS

XII POEMS OF CONTINUING CONNECTION

Introduction

When, at the age of 81, I decided to cut the tangled threads of attachment that had marooned me in an old people's enclave of tiny bungalows in Kessingland, Suffolk, UK, little did I anticipate the dramatic changes that decision would bring to my exterior and interior landscapes.

This book of poems is the outcome of the most dynamic, transforming and creative seven years of my life. It no longer surprises me that its formulation owes so much to the turbulent unfolding of a new paradigm forged by the smouldering passions of post-Apartheid South Africa in these early shape-shifting years of a third millennium.

Here, in the clamorous intermingling of cultures and races in the burgeoning, little-known suburb of Fish Hoek on the coast of Cape Town's False Bay, I have become part of an exciting and often challenging metamorphosis, a sea-change of outer and inner perspectives that has inevitably followed Nelson Mandela's *Long Walk to Freedom*.

And not only here in South Africa.

Is there one in all the world who has not trembled before the seeming chaos precipitated by rapid change?

It has been my pleasure to try and capture the essence that pervades this era of constant flux in cameos of my own experience of fleeting Moments of Time.

In doing this, I imply a linear time-scale in the ordering of the twelve sections from 1, 'Poems of Place', to 12. 'Poems of Continuing Connection', but the poems themselves have been allocated to one or other section emphasis or theme irrespective of the poem's biographical genesis. In this way I hope they may reflect our alternating shifts of attention to Past, Present and Future that features so much in our transient lives at this time.

The poems of *Not More of the Same* plead for readiness to let go of outward, moribund forms of being and for openness to the influx of energy pulses that would have us prepare inwardly for the needs of the Age of Aquarius.

Then we shall find respite, although only briefly, for all our arrivals are also points of departure.

Lewis Watling
Fish Hoek. April 2008

I

Poems of Place

When You Can Hear a Pin Drop

Having lived in England, Canada and South Africa and having served with the RAF in France and also South Africa, I have developed a deep awareness of the Spirit of Place.

I have never felt this more intensively than when I returned to Meadow River, in Northern Saskatchewan, for a reunion celebration of the small rural school of which I had been principal back in the 1950s. So let me share with you a little cameo:

After two days of outdoor activities all the folk who had returned to this place of their nurturing had assembled in the old schoolroom at Bear Creek for a Saturday night Barn Dance.

There, in my late seventies, I sat and revelled in the energies released by the racing fiddles and watched the class of '56 gyrate around the dance floor. Late in the evening the Meadow Lake Senator who had been largely responsible for arranging the weekend programme came across and sat on the empty chair beside me.

"Lewis," he said as soon as the fiddles gave him a chance to make his voice heard, "I wonder if you could do us a favour?"

"OK" I wasn't too sure what I was letting myself in for, but what the heck, I was on holiday and among old friends. I raised my eyebrows quizzically.

"I've just heard that the pastor who was going to take our Sunday morning worship tomorrow is unable to be here. Could you fill in for him?"

I scratched the back of my head. How could I explain that after ten years as a Methodist lay preacher in Britain I'd had a crisis of faith in the authenticity and effectiveness of orthodox religion, and had taken a solemn vow never to speak from a pulpit again.

"It does pose a bit of a problem," I replied. "Can you give me a half hour or so to think it through? I'll let you know before the night is out."

And there I sat, the music and the drums calling to me through some kind of primal imagery. Consolidate the bonds of friendship, or hold true to my own integrity?

After half an hour I had made up my mind and, when the music stopped, I slipped over to where the Senator sat with his party.

Very briefly I explained my dilemma: "I am honoured that you should ask me," I said, "but I can only say yes if you agree that I take the service in the form of Quaker Silent Worship."

He placed a hand on my shoulder without giving me a chance to elaborate further. "Anything... anything...," he murmured. "And thank you. I don't know what else we could have done."

Thus it was on Sunday morning I introduced the good folk of Meadow River District to the ways of Quaker Worship, seeking to facilitate their participation by focusing their attention upon four realms of the spirit, each to be followed by a relatively short period of silence in which anyone was free to minister if they so wished. The topics were: 1. Spirit of Place, 2. Spirit of Community, 3. Spirit of Ancestors and 4. Spirit of Love.

Nobody volunteered any verbal contribution and the final period of silence was just about through when Mike Kulchuski, a wizened old Ukrainian farmer, climbed to his feet.

"It ain't often," he intoned, "us Northlanders git together an' you kin hear a pin drop."

Not all the poems in this section are occasions for hearing a pin drop, but the same spirit is to be found in each of them.

This was the poem I had written to take to folk I had not seen and had only had infrequent contact with over forty years:

Meadow River 1997

I am come among strangers.

Oh, I remember nineteen-fifty-four
when the earth road slid into the creek,
and the only road to town lay
through the Reservation.
Ernest Nault's caboose
spat spray from surface run-off
to bring us tales of chaos
as we picked raspberries from flooded canes
behind the Autocourt.

You made us welcome then.
We had arrived, an English family,
tossed by post-war tumult
into cross-Atlantic flight,
wary as beavers;
not that we knew a darned sight
about them, or this northern wilderness,
its even stranger folk;
the four of us (our children: six and two).
And I had come to teach you?

Meadow River!
The name dripped images of rural bliss,
not crevasses of mud,
white water in V-ditches,
sodden overshoes, earth closets
and August's rich
sprinkling of early snow.

I have photographs to show
I don't exaggerate.
That year snow poked drifting fingers
deep into the quarter sections
of late-ripening grain.

And now I've come again
– because I wish to reconcile
that once unfriendly landscape
with the warmth still stored
here in my memories of Meadow River folk
through the long years.

Where do I start to tell my story?
With Hallowe'en antics, and Lena's pumpkin pie?
the cries of laughing girls
strutting the butterfly dance
to racing fiddles in the Junior Room?
No; more personal than that.
In my mind's eye, I see
Marlene and Elaine wind up the gramophone,
gyrate, weave, sway,
cry "Holy Smoke!" and "Holy Cow!",
their youthful limbs the slaves
of the Once-Now;
Jimmy Ludwig and the young Ouellettes
upon their horse-drawn sleighs
laughing their way to school?
Brian Ludwig, one day
the only child bucking curving drifts
(He only stayed with me
to shovel white-stuff until lunchtime)?
Lorraine and Sandra carrying
the Meadow River banner in the Meadow Lake parade?
What made this tapestry so rich?

Not just the school's children:
Christine, Lorna, Lawrence, Carol Ann,
Darlene, Olive, Glenn,
Vivian, the Alberts, Lenkos,
Kenny and occasional nomads
from Peace River country.
Over two years their families would invite
these upstart foreigners for a Sunday meal.
And not just them: Shorty Peters and Mike Kulchuski
had no kids at school but joined the band;
and Mike Belik ploughed a strip of land
for me to garden.
It seemed to stretch for miles!

Yes, I recall a place
of friendship, families and smiles,
an oasis of grace;
although our Sandra, nearing fifty now,
and friend of rabbits, ponies, spiders, snails,
has been afraid of turkeys ever since
she lunched at Mary Gehl's.
She sends her love.

All this my tangled memory threads recall.
I could go on, but here this story ends.
Those kids – they're nearer sixty now
than to sweet sixteen which once they were,
that time you took us in to heart and home.
The long years since change nothing deep within.

No, it's not to strangers that I come,
But old and trusted friends.

The Canadian experience enabled me to realize that no matter where we venture we take our baggage with us. After I returned to Norfolk the baggage became burdensome and my marriage of 23 years came to an end. With my possessions reduced to a car and two suitcases I set out across the Norfolk border into Suffolk. The move liberated my poet's voice, and I became involved with the "Bungay Poets". For a while, I experimented with dialect poems. This poem appeared as the final poem in "Poet's England – 15 – Suffolk", Brentham Press, 1994.

Border Country

Thass wholly different from where I used to live,
here, acrorst the Waveney?
where they talk Silly Suffolk an' arsk
a question ev'ry toime they speak? –
Moind yew, Oi allus hankered after Border Country.
Even as a Norfolk Dumplin' bucklin' ter the task
of ekin' out a living, Oi would squint
acrorst the river an' wonder why Oi din't
tear up my roots an' move.
Some things have a need fer careful statin',
an' Oi loiked the haveri', the gentle touch…
not that they need ter sing or mardle on so much.
An' yit,
since I come parst the river just a little way
Oi've got more used ter waitin'
afore Oi haven my say.
It's almost loike Oi've softened up a bit,
made way fer them that's not the same as me.
That's it!
Yew have ter take your toime in Border Country.

I thought I'd found my final home in Suffolk when, after ten years in Kirby Cane, ten years in Beccles and a further ten years in Kessingland, I visited my youngest daughter, Maria, who was then living with her mother and stepfather in Cape Town. They took me to Cape Point and the experience produced this Poem of Place and had me thinking about relocating yet again.

Cape Point – New Year's Day 1998

The pamphlet had said it was the centenary
of the sinking of the Nuktaris
in Baffles Bay, with four men dead....
At the foot of Cape Point's Lighthouse,
sporting shorts, white shirt, straw hat,
the tourist sat, his thoughts far, far away.

With Khoisan laughter making sea-music
of the day's brightness,
two sisters play,
one four, the other twelve, perhaps,
their mother safely near.
"Here comes the demon
to take you away!"
The eyes of one light up with love,
the other's flash mock fear.

Oh! The wonder
as the old man nods his head,
adrift on other seas
and under cloudier skies.
"Wait!" the mother cries,
"my skatjies, let me take a photograph."

Arousing from a blanket
of lazing, dozing, browsing,

the old man stoops to move his bag
and shift himself.

"No! Let things be," the mother laughs.
"We're all in it together,
– part of the scenery."

In 2001 I became a permanent South African resident. 3 years later Maria's partner was killed in a car crash. With her infant son, we took a holiday in Southern Cross. This poem was written for Nellie and Herman Massyn, Maria's partner's parents.

Beach House, Southern Cross

We come, raw with the wounds of Life,
to find a balm
not only of sand and sea,
but hearts wide open
to the capricious tides that run
ceaselessly beneath this surface calm.
Like carefree children
we dance the sparkling waves,
laugh at the way they fling us casually
this way and that, heedless of human dreams,
our cares adrift upon a cosmic flow
and, just when beauty's everything it seems,
we feel the savage power
of a dread undertow.
In that dark hour we need to hold a hand,
to find the shelter of an open heart,
to feel firm foothold on the shifting sand,
discover this is **not** a place apart.
And even if the heavens far above
seem starless, inner pain supreme,
nightmares feature in the place of dream,
here, with the healing touch of sun and sea
and gentle heart, we shall remember
this is a place of love.

My first experience of participating in a dawn Easter vigil, a typical outdoor celebration in the sun-kissed Cape, with folk other than with near family, had been with three Quaker friends. We met on Fisherman's Beach, Simon's Town, on Easter Sunday 2002. It was a memorable experience of a very special place.

Fisherman's Beach

Wool-wrapped against the wind, we four
had risen early to seek an Easter dawn.
We sat there silently upon that grass-capped earth
now autumn-thatched, but still shading to green,
and yielded to the smiling sun's rebirth.
Beneath a fading moon, the ocean penned
long, ink-stained ripples endlessly,
great whorls of interwoven consequence
criss-crossed by counter force from rocky shore.
More cryptic still,
As mountain crests caught fire,
the new dawn's searching rays edged glacial white
each seventh wave
to crash and splash upon
impediment,
its sparkling foam hurled high by cleansing wind
before it found again its former home.

Shore birds awoke
and winged their proven way
to seek their daily harvest from the sea's vast store,
careless of Easter ritual.
An early walker threw a coil of kelp
to launch the dawn companion of his day
into the restless flow.
Again... again... again...
until the moment when

the quarry disappeared in some strange undertow.
They shrugged incomprehension, strolled away.

We watched the rising sun,
each with unspoken thoughts, until
with sea-washed bough,
one traced a labyrinth on the gleaming sand.
We edged our way along
its convolutions to the centre, where
we listened to the strong, clear warning
in the wild waves' cry.

These things we see, the How of everyday,
do they not remind us of the Why?
I knew dark night had gone, but still
I could not write
the sad sea's song.

On Easter Sunday three years later the vigil experience was repeated and triggered the following poem.

Easter Sunday 2005

New friends – Zimbabwean visitors –
wrapped in winter garb against the chill
joined us for our Easter ritual.
Silently we sat, newly remembering
the age-old tidal pull
of sun and moon;
felt tremors as our body cells, awakening,
recalled a story that cannot be told
about the living universe. The distant cloud-bank rolled,
and soon
a fissure in its canopy caught fire
only to fade, turn grey, then yield to gold.

Bathed in new light, our hearts awoke
to inner rhythms of an ancient birth.
Briefly we saw and felt the world-soul of Sophia,
font of wisdom, matrix of our earth.

When from the rapture of this haunting hour
we stretched ourselves, with shaft of kelp as pen,
once more our artist re-sketched her labyrinth on sand,
and we retraced those inward steps again
to the heart-centre. It was then
that I began to understand:
Sophia hides a Wisdom beyond this reign of men
as yet unfashioned, unfinished and unplanned.

Oh! how our hearts await the guidance of her hand!

Five years after settling in the flat under the little school in St. James
that my daughter, and her mother and stepfather administered, and
to which I added my own teaching skills, I yielded to the physical
discomfort of negotiating 115 mountainside steps upon arriving or
leaving my flat to shop, to post a letter, or to be ferried to some event or
pastime.
    Once again I uprooted and relocated. Determined to be self-sufficient
and able to meet all my major requirements on foot, I moved into a flat
in Fish Hoek. Within a few months of being there I was asked by Viv
von der Heydn, joint proprietor of Fish Hoek Printing, if I would write
a poem for her proposed annual information booklet, Fish Hoek Valley
in Focus. *This was the poem that resulted:*

Fish Hoek – A Habitat For Happiness

Towards Community

I little dreamed, when I began to write
the earlier chapters of my lifetime book,
that I would end this dance through earth-screened light
in far Fish Hoek,
or, that my heart would ride the valley wind,
my old legs stride these sparkling strands and hills
around a bay where, swift and silver-finned,
the Great White kills.

Here, where eagles wing on thermal flow,
and leopard-toads warble their drenched delight
in wetland reed-beds, where Orion's faithful glow
enchants the night,
I talk with geese, converse with guinea fowl,
negotiate with rock-doves, pigeons, butterflies,
track mountain pathways where wild creatures prowl,
baboons surprise.
Still, in the bustling town, and slow to grow,
old phantoms of past violence glide and slink,

not bold enough to let the old ways go,
new ways to think.
But, working, playing, living side by side
in school and church and restaurant and store,
the rainbow insights have nowhere to hide
and more and more

the bright threads intertwine in patterns that
contrive to mould and modify and bless
a new Fish Hoek – a model habitat
for happiness.
In my last years, it deeply pleases me
that through the dark I've journeyed on to see
and join this walk towards a shared ideal.
– Community.

Having dipped my poet's toe into the special mix of Fish Hoek's gifts of community, it became somewhat a perennial habit to write a poem for the annual booklet. This was my offering for 2007:

Aka Fish Hoek

There's a bustling little suburb on the coast road round False Bay
(Are you one of those who never stop to look?)
where initiatives are spilling – democratic, so they say –
to add more scenes of beauty to the pictures in this book.
And although we are reputed to be unusual and fey,
dowdy and old-fashioned, and featureless and grey,
it's here we come together on our enterprises daily
from all the fringe communities, like Masiphumelele,
and it's really very splendid in a special sort of way:
this place of many churches – aka Fish Hoek.

A multitude of pigeons have made themselves at home
(their feral broods are found in every nook,
each with patterned wings and tail, like some senescent gnome,
though silent as old phantoms from an other-worldly book.
Their half-wild cousins are the ones who serenade the dawn,
and croon unceasing to the sun their joy at being born).
Can it be such creatures in their domesticity
are simulating in their way our own duplicity
and go about their annual task – to find a mate and spawn
the bird-plebs of Pigeonville – aka Fish Hoek?

And what of us, the common folk of this outspreading town,
(the Hickville that the new Capetonians forsook)?
Are we tainted by the image of the old and tumble-down,
or, should the experts take another look?
We've something good to offer – a multi-cultured mix,
a melting pot in which to brew our many human tricks,
and learn the ways to trust and honour each one's special talent,

discover ways of being that are courteous and gallant.
We're not just single-minded, doing our own things for kicks,
but building a new Valley Land – aka Fish Hoek.

I love to stroll its busy streets now I am eighty-seven
to buy the simple things I need, and do it all on foot
unaffected by the anger and hate of 9/11;
the day when the foundations of all our systems shook.
A new domain awaits you... and you... and you... and you.
It needs your light, integrity, the fruits of being true
to your deepest knowledge of your own humanity
to help this sorry world of ours regain its soul and sanity.
All it needs is power from the courageous few
to grow again this crystal glen – aka Fish Hoek.

II
Poems for People

For ten years towards the end of my teaching career I was teaching very young children with learning difficulties. At least that was how my task was described in the educational techno-speak of the time.

It was not until I retired and found time for reflection that the realization of what was actually occurring began to dawn. Those children – Rachel, Beverley, Sarah, Julie, Stephen, Anthony, Blaine – with their gifts of handicap were as much my instructors as I theirs.

They all featured in the thesis on self-esteem that I presented at the Cambridge Institute of Education in 1976.

Danny Jeffrey was a Down's syndrome child, then six years old, now forty-six. The first poem in the section tells of his early years and his family background, and the beginning of a life story that is a parable of courage and innocence.

He lived with his mother and four siblings, each older than Danny, on a permanent caravan site in Belton, near Great Yarmouth. His was the first home I visited in pursuit of a dream; a dream that involved the full constellation of the family in any healing work that might ensue.

Only his dad no longer played a part in his life.

Joyce, Danny's mum, has, ever since that first visit, never failed to connect me with him on the occasion of his or my birthdays and at Christmas.

But it was not until he spoke to me over the phone on my seventy-first birthday and said, "I love you, Mr. Watlin'," that the beautiful clarity of spontaneous expression pierced the defences of my heart.

Since then I have been able to write many poems for many people, some of which appear in this collection, and I have learned that we receive back into ourselves the mirror image of what we have ourselves projected.

Thank you Danny, Joyce, Lenny, Jean, Lynn, David for teaching me that invaluable lesson.

Here is the poem I wrote for Danny when he was six years old.

Danny Jeffrey

Your eyes were scuttling grey spiders
dancing on silken threads
of thoughts unspoken.
Sometimes you grumbled
beneath your breath
vague monosyllables of dissent,
as if your heart lay pierced and broken
by the burden of so cruel a fate.
Back in the village
your mother would await
each school-day's end
when Jean and Lenny, Lynn and David,
maybe a friend and you would clatter in
to rock the caravan that served as home;
and then you'd sing, though not in tune,
and everything,
though cramped, seemed cosy.
In Norfolk's wintry eastern chill
your breath would falter,
mucus block your nose,
and you'd be ill
for ages.
Yet still you laughed (not one real tear I saw
in fifteen months of knowing your delight).
Nor were you angry, though sometimes in the war
of selves that throbbed within the school
you'd drop your pants and grimace, spreading fright
in those whose teasing pride deemed you the fool.
And now and then
your wandering eyes would rest,
your limbs grow still again,

your hand steal low
upon my arm, and you would crow
contentedly. Your lips would brush my cheek,
your hand caress, and so
I watched you grow
I watched you grow.

For Saffyre Malherbe, (who shared much learning time with me in the little Raphael Home School in St. James).

Shared Awakenings

Sixteen!
Oh! how the world quakes!
The unlived years
unloose their unformed shapes
to haunt your dream-time ceaselessly.
Hormones, are blamed, or growing pains,
or teenage angst which sparks the rage and tears,
veiling the golden world you long to build.
Expel these fleeting fears.
For all the things that you already *know*
are timeless, spirit-given, soul-designed
to nurture love, enable you to grow,
and release Light until your doubts are stilled.
Will you remember, when you reach for home,
these times we shared –
the sadness and the joy; the love; the trust;
the tricks that numbers play; the times we dared
to chuckle at the madness of the half-awake;
Will's and Lyra's battles for the Shadow-Dust;
our radiant counterparts in Beauty's Lake;
unnamed poets, philosophers and writers
(as well as Shakespeare, Pullman, Tolkien, Aristotle);
the precedents of history's greatest fighters;
the forever-secrets of the body's power,
breathing and sound; drama; the farewell hug;
and, not least, the comfort of the old hot-water bottle.

This was written for four-year-old Rain whose mother took part in an energy sharing session that I had been invited to attend in 2006.

A Prayer for Rain

Let's quit awhile the zone of sacred sound
where cosmic music casts its spell upon
our inward ear, and utilize the lexicon
of science.
Let's talk *codon*.
The white-coats found
that sixty-four genetic patterns stem
from nucleic acids in our DNA.
But, of them,
only twenty are "switched on", they say.

And then... and then...
one of the Indigos at birth
showed twenty-four such sequences that shone!
resisted death diseases on our present earth,
and could switch on
for those with whom they'd briefly stay
their new codons.

Now, back to Indigo:
It's New Year's Eve, and we met to share
the annual round of New Year resolutions;
one young Mum, five middle-mogs, an oldie
and a four-year-old,
and she – her name was Rain –
eyes brown, hair gold, but clearly Indigo,
spilled shards of morphic sensors through
the seasonal pollutions
that had beguiled our gathered throng.

Soon Rain found the resonance she sought,
maternal wisdom that could sing her infant song.
She hitched herself to Astrid, who caught
her need, shape-shifted, and became
the doppelgänger in her little game;
giggled, tickled, jiggled, let her hide
beneath the table, coming up to play
at being grown up – clink glasses for a toast –
until, child-energy dispersed, she sighed,
gave way to sleep, and lay
upon the couch.

Raging through the nights since Christmas Day,
the fires that purge the mountains of the Western Cape
also await another energy to cool their hungry flames.
Let us unhook the tentacles of yesterday:
distorted visions of a false supremacy;
old, imagined legacies of hate and pain;
outgrown rituals of our New Year games;
and fashion, not just with our thoughts, but with our acts,
new ways to be -
and love's true prayer for Rain.

For Astrid on her 50th birthday (August 22nd, 2006). Astrid was the mother of Saffyre Malherbe whom it was my privilege to teach in the Raphael Home School in St. James from 2002 onwards. That we had become firm friends was due, I believe, to some existing unseen bond between us that was to continue to flourish throughout my remaining years.

Half-Way

"It IS, just IS."
so the mantra flows.
Thus we pollute potential,
limit expectation, filter out the fizz
of sunflower, lily, carnation, daisy, rose,
the vital stuff of self and all that grows.

And fifty is *your* IS –
or IS IT?
Who are you? Mrs? Miss? or Ms?
Astrid, the toddler? Teenage tear-about?
Kibbutz crusader? Or discombobulated Mum?
Or all of these – and more –
what you must still become?

I cannot transplant you to a place
that's nearer one hundred than halfway,
although I've tried. No need to spout
these words in verse. You *know* already.

And when the heart is calm, the pulse-rate steady,
and you have shed the last desire,
there will remain a lambent, perfect core,
the jewel of your own life-fire.

For Ceara East: Ceara was the second daughter of a family of two girls and three boys, the offspring of Jacqui Cawkwell-East, a Quaker Friend in Suffolk, U.K. Ceara was first wheeled into my life when she was two, and I became a kind of surrogate granddad for her whole family. In her gap year between school and university, she decided to call in and spend time with me in Cape Town on her return trip from India where she had been doing voluntary service, teaching English as a foreign language.

Midwinter in The Cape of Storms

You came,
a speck of animated stardust
sizzling with Suffolk grace,
new Indian spice
and flavours of Natal,
though still a trace
of patient, pastoral Peasenhall
shone through.

How the heart warms
when a familiar face
conjures memories of another time,
another place!
And so it was
as we sat out
the blasts of Winter
in the Cape of Storms.

Yet, when the sun shone
we walked,
and when it didn't,
talked… and talked… and talked…
Deep, deep, deep, we trawled the realm of soul,
the breadth of human folly, and everything between.

("I'm not sure I believe in a Supreme Being,"
you said – at just nineteen!)

And then, that star-burst Sunday:
Astrid, Saffyre, you and I
sharing lunch with gulls,
and laughing at the fun-day
promise of two pink girls –
or were they puppets being jerked by strings
near Camps Bay beach?

Driving halfway to the sky
to find the cable-way shut down,
we chose to tread the mountainside,
skirting rock-falls, trickling down-flows,
hikers, bikers, on the scenic roadway
sealed from cars, to savour vibrant vistas
of Cape Town's glorious, global, vibrant city-bowl.

Elsewhere, you also found the time
sometimes alone, sometimes with me, to sample other scenes:
Jager's Walk, the southern end of Fish Hoek's beach
towards Glencairn; wetlands of Silvermine
beneath Clovelly Heights; penguins at Boulders; quaint Kalk Bay
(While we were there I gave you quite a scare
by fainting in the search for curios,
but I was not ready to be one of those!)

On Saturday we took the Metro for Muizenberg's Theatre,
fed up with waiting for the sun to shine!

I'm glad you came. Better
gifts than these will never honour me:
your bubbling youth, your easy ways, your energy,
not least, your love of reading;
so may I borrow words from *Little Tree* to say:
"I kin ye, Ceara East."

*For Diane Salters and Peter Willis (regular hosts of Quaker House
Meetings in the Cape's Southern Peninsula. I was invited to their
home after refurbishment and met Paul Mason and Silke Heiss, who
introduced me to Hugh Hodge's "Off The Wall" Open Mike Poetry
Sessions in Observatory).*

The Housewarming

What makes a house a home?
– that place of Robert Frost's, where the heart is,
where you are taken in?
or Edward Thomas's – where
"All was foretold me, naught
could I foresee,
but I learned how the wind would sound
after these things should be."
– or Bertholt Brecht –
"Every day, as I drive through the ruins, I am reminded
of the privileges to which I owe this house. I hope
it will not make me patient with the holes
in which so many thousands huddle."
– or Robert Crawford – "Home
is where we hang up our clothes and costumes
without thought."
– or Gerard Manley Hopkins –
"Come you indoors, come home, your fading fire
mend first, and vital candle to heart's vault."
– or Sophie Hannah –
"If their affair has awkward spells
what's bound to cause the rows is
that he treats houses like hotels,
and she hotels like houses."
– or Philip Larkin – whose home is sad and
"turns again to what it started as.
a joyous shot at how things ought to be."

– or Christina Rosetti –
"When I was dead, my spirit turned
To seek the much frequented house,
I passed the door and saw my friends
Feasting beneath green orange boughs;
From hand to hand they pushed the wine.
They sucked the pulp of plum and peach.
They sang, they jested, and they laughed,
For each was loved of each."

And what say I?
I, who was taken in,
who, in age, foresees
what after things shall be?
who learned to reach,
in true compassion to millions in their holes?
and how, through difference, we can learn to be
each loved of each?

I say that it was warm, this home,
not because of all the beauteous things
it holds within
– mementoes of John Keats's joy forever –
but for those unmasked moments of reality
when seeking minds and unclosed hearts
were met together
to share the mystery of what it is
to live and Be.

For Michael Copley: Mike was a poet, singer, guitar player and song writer who led a poetry group in Muizenberg when I first came to Cape Town in 2001.

The Radiant Folk

Once in a while, they burst into our lives,
The radiant folk, trailing cosmic glory.
Larger than life, they batter down
the gaol-house of our reticence
to liberate the soul in our life-story.
Mix of actor, minstrel, mystic, clown,
poet, guide and friend,
they conjure visions of a world to be.
When we hear their haunting songs
that tell of life that's lived,
of gifts received and shared,
of old Earth's secret rhapsodies,
of blessing, knowledge, wonder without end,
upon the whispering wind we hear
the messages of trees.

For Ivan Massyn (my daughter's partner) during his pilot training sessions.

Smooth Landings

I cannot fly you to that rare altitude
where legs and feet and toes
refuse at last the comfort of the fecund earth.
for all must go there solo;
not for us to choose the landing strip,
the talk-down, or the wind's upthrust.

That's why
on every flight
and every day
we have to yield a little of the "I".
"Amen!" you wrote, searching your poet soul,
"A man needs other men, especially older men
to bless him and to honour him;
to encourage, to point out his mistakes,
and to raise his status."
Thus you analysed your manhood's goal.

Sure, man must fly his culture's ordinance
but, to reach the sky
and the rhythms of a whole universe,
he can't too readily forsake
the hidden gift that craves an understanding:
his mother's heart feeding a nascent love;
for, if he does, he'll find it hard to die,
and – worse –
he'll never make smooth landing.

For Gillian Hawkes and her friend, Lynn: Gillian is a Southern Peninsular Quaker.

The Watchers: Tracking McNaught's Comet (19.01.2007)

A January Friday near Kommetjie;
the sun had slipped behind
a ribboned cloud on the horizon rim
as the Atlantic paled in shadow and we,
uncertain watchers, scanned the now dim
afterglow of sunset for our first view of it.
A dozen car-borne amateurs like us
were parked nearby,
eyes riveted upon the darkening sky.
But – nothing… nothing… nothing…
And soon our human counterfeit of Time
would urge us quit.
Then, all at once, a golden orb
descended slowly, vertically,
a spreading, fiery tail and in the lingering flush
of western light
Hierophany!

How tiny are our selves, feeble the flame
that would ignite the sacred in our Being
and how readily we played the watching game
expecting satisfaction just through *seeing.*
As we watched we sensed another story,
a scripted narrative of galaxy and star
and, even when late-coming headlights outshone the comet's glory,
we clung to intimations beamed us from afar.
How immense they seemed, those wonders and that ecstasy,
the very stuff of comet engulfing you and me.

For Ralph Shepherd, Director of the Novalis College and Institute, on his 60th birthday.

Novalis Ubuntu

Always…
Always you dreamed a dream
of some far shore
where, altogether, we might learn how to restore
within the humdrum of our daily lives
the distant drumming of another way,
and so, bring into play the poet's power
of myth and mood and metaphor.

Remember how
that vision held through long, tormented years,
through pain of war, through bleak apartheid fears,
to help rebuild a shining rainbow hope?
Then again the tears
of widespread AIDS?

And now,
caught in the sickness of this toxic March,
two million crayfish flee the inert foam,
preferring death to long, slow suffering?

May we, like them, like you, forever sing
and dare in our own lives your heartfelt prayer:
Nkosi sikelel' iAfrika!

For always… always… always…
you've been coming Home.

III

PASTORAL POEMS

Hev Yew Ever Seen a Daisy Wink?

The sense of being a divided self has been with me most of my life. Part of me has never failed to wonder at the sheer magnificence of Nature and, awed by its multiplicity of form, its breathtaking synergies of connection and its harmonies of design and function, has been ever ready to bow before the great god, Pan.

Then, becoming aware of what to human perception appears to be a massive indifference when Fire, Water, Air or Earth reveal their essence *in extremis* as in volcano, flood, tornado and earthquake, I am drawn back into a search for the gods and goddesses of humankind whose ordinances run into millions of words the world over, and promise eternal deliverance from the mind's sense of suffering and loss.

And then the excessive zeal that would achieve this ideal "on earth as it is in heaven", by eliminating the purveyors of any different orthodoxy, return me to seek solace in the realms of Nature again, where the carnage is, at least, not usually pre-emptive.

It was back in 1997, before my ambivalence was put to the test in Meadow River, that I was drawn into the presentation of an evening of poetry and music by a group of West-End actors and actresses, one of whose number had fled the city and taken refuge in the Suffolk village of Peasenhall. There, among a number of artistes who included Alan Bates and Maggie Steed, my dialect poem, "Hev Yew Ever Seen a Daisy Wink?" appeared on the programme, its title followed by "read by himself".

Like other poems in this section "Hev Yew Ever Seen a Daisy Wink?" echoes the paradox of today's quantum physics: it is not possible to describe the forms that the energy of Light makes manifest when attempting such description **either** as physical particles **or** as waves of energy; veracity acknowledging the necessity for both. Hence the validation of both the poet's metaphors **and** the scientist's formulaic ordering.

So, Truth-Seeker, consider well if it is you or the daisy actually **doing** the winking.

Hev Yew Ever Seen a Daisy Wink?

Hev yew ever seen a daisy wink?
Not knowingly like, but quick,
hidin' her yeller eye
under pink lashes
when Roger's Blast spanks by.

Sometimes, with all her mates,
she'll gently nod,
an' toss a sight o' sunbeams
from the grass sod
to nurture bright dreams.

Always, I think,
she'll turn her head away
from any hoity-toity talk
of a tall neighbour
on a plumpendicular stalk.

But she's there for yew
on any Summer walk,
or on your lawn,
to nod and smile and blink
– if the grass ain't shorn,
an' yew can match her wink.

As a boy I used to spend my Summer holidays on my Uncle Jack's farm where, for three years from the time I was nine, I was Hold-Ye Boy for the duration of the harvest. In the 1980's I tried to recapture the magic and bliss of those days and the nuances of the Norfolk dialect. This is the first of two such poems that I broadcasted on Radio Suffolk, but I did not continue the practice because using a full dialect made them unintelligible to many of the listeners.

Hold-Ye, Hold-Ye Tight

When I look for memories to lift a lonely heart
I call to mind a sparkling day in Suffolk – carting oats.
I remember it was a bit of a scorcher
with the sun sizzling our sweat
faster than we could slake our thirst
with bottles of cold tea
and the dust on the thirty-acre
coated our lips each time a sheaf was hurled.
There was Arnie, Dodger – and me
riding the Suffolks between the shafts.
Arnie was pitcher, Dodger rode and loaded,
and that oat-field was our world.
I was only a littl'un,
ten maybe, but I knew my stuff,
hollering, "Hold-Ye!" on cue.
You had to get it right
or the loader might
have landed on Arnie's pitch-fork.
And I allowed just far enough
to guide the wagon from the stooks
so Arnie didn't have to walk
and waste his muscle-power.

You should have seen Prince race along
to the stack-yard with our last load

in the blue twilight hour!
That field of gold was where I grew
into the ranks of men
and harvested the gifts of team-work.
Now memory's all that's left, and when
I ride my lonely wagon homeward for the night
my phantoms holler loud: "Hold-Ye! Hold-Ye Tight!"

And here's another one about those times.

Trace Horse

Three harvests I rode the Suffolks
hollering, "Hold-Ye!"
Ineffable it was
to feel the trust of two grown men
in such a tiny foreigner.
By the time I was thirteen,
I knew every each whisker
on Prince's chin
and how to squiggle when barley harns
prickled my skin all pins-and-needles.
You can guess what came into my head
when my Uncle Jack said,
"Your cousin Giles is here.
He'll be riding 'Hold-Ye' this year."
I wondered what I'd done.
I'd never tipped old Dodger off the load,
and Arnie reckoned I was as good
as anyone they'd had before.
My Uncle smiled, "You're no but a child,"
he said, "but I think you'll fill a gap.
How do you fancy the trace horse?"
I gaped, Me? Hitching the extra horse
to drag the wagons up Hill Meadow and then
riding bareback down the hill again?
Cor! My Christmas had come in August!
"You have to be wide awake," my Uncle said,
"There ain't much time for sleeping on the long rein."

"Cumather!" I hollered, coming through the gate
to the stack-yard. And, "Wurr-de-whisk!"
in real good time so's not to risk
getting to the stack on skew.

I did it well.
I'd unhitch the horse, toss the long rein
around her collar, lift the draw-bar,
climb on her back beside the ladder
and canter like Hell down the long hill.
Only once did she turn her head
and roll her eyes at me.
I was so tired I couldn't hold up the bar
and it cut hard against her thighs.
Although she larded up a bit, I rubbed her down
and, come nightfall, she looked as slick as ever;
her coat a-shine like Sunday shoes,
her mane afire, her heart too proud
to wilt or tire.

Sometimes I wonder who taught whom,
for down the years in my mind's eye
I've often cantered bareback down that hill
and often had her hitched before my wagon
when the going's glum.
She was a rare, fine horse, a proper chum
to me. Her name was Beauty.

Suffolk Dialect Words
Cumather: Order to turn left
Wurr-de-whisk: Order to turn right

When putting the sections of Not More of the Same *together I almost allocated this one to the "Poems for People" section; but then I figured Astrid has her share of praise elsewhere and the forest sprites and their pastoral presence deserve affirmation too.*

Tokai Arboretum

Rare summer rain had primed the forest sprites
to wear their finest raiment on a sparkling day.
Such were their heady welcomes
as we picked our steady way
by rock and root and mud-hole;
through gulleys, tunnelled trees
that no past half-seen fancy
could ever rival these.
We walked and talked, fell silent,
awed by this vast display.
Remember how, like children,
we paused to stare and say
what images we saw within a tree-framed, craggy stone
whose unscreened earth-bound energy
spoke to our deep Alone?

There, on a dipping pathway
to prevent a sudden fall
our fingers signaled mindfulness
of life-breath, heartbeat…All…
as down… down… down… we ventured
into a deep, green calm.
Once there, we sought permission
to take a token charm;
called thanks to the top branches
for the oak leaf I'd plucked free,
when there came a sudden movement
in the top twigs of the tree.

A wayward breeze caressed them,
as if its spirit cried
in febrile exultation,
and all the forest sighed.

When the sensations weaken
will you still stroll with me
to the music of the forest,
the whispering of a tree
or will you just remember
the scone with cream and tea?

This is another one in which the gifts of Astrid and the forest merged:

Elephant's Ears

"There is no going back," I said
as we slipped into the forest,
our memories
stirred by its green stillness,
images from startling rocks,
dream-time ballads of droning bumble bees,
the murmuring tales of trees.
I dare not hope for further re-cognition.
Fool!
Why should they repeat heart messages
unheard?

And then… and then…

This time we climbed to higher planes,
until we came to sit upon a rock –
a base for clustered rocks –
which patiently endured our dualogue
(though, sometimes, we also shared their silences).
The afternoon's late shadows cooled our tongues,
and, as we rose to go,
you gave our thanks for stones.
I laid my palm against the weathered grain
and felt, and saw, and knew the source again.
"Like Rodin's Thinker.
No! Rather the Silent Listener," I said,
pointing to the contours and remembering
the constant, inward promptings of the years.
And you, your heart's voice monitoring your head,
deemed these listening forms:
"Huge! Just like an elephant's ears."

Links with the natural world were never severed, even in the most testing times. "Dawn Voices" was written some years before I leapfrogged to South Africa, imagining myself in my little "senior citizen's" bungalow in Kessingland to be firmly ensconced in the ultimate dwelling place of this life-journey.

Dawn Voices

This morning in the Owl hours I remembered
those Spring awakenings of long, long, long ago
when pre-dawn loosed a Hallelujah chorus
chirruped by warbler, wagtail, finch and sparrow
in counterpoint to a far cockerel's crow.
The prelude came from stuttering yellow-hammer,
the rhapsody from robin, wren and lark,
solo from song thrush, till it paused in song-burst
to drum a snail's shell on a random rock.
And then I wondered why a single blackbird,
muffled, distant, lone, left me amazed
to hear how muted was the cosmic echo,
how soul-sick was the dawn when few birds sing.

Of course I know my closet's double-glazed!

While in my Kessingland bungalow I used to keep a store of Milky Way chocolate bars that I doled out to passing children. Their presence at my front door led me to write this poem. It received an Ottakar Bookzshop award for National Poetry Day, 1998.

Sunflower Seeds

When I am very old
(say ninety-four)
I'll plant a special seed
by my front door
so children come to sit or play,
their eyes ablaze with wonder
at the reach of it.

Somewhere indoors,
towards the end
of more-than-forty winks
I'll hear their laughter
and I'll shuffle out.
They'll leave its shade
and hold a golden buttercup
beneath my chin,
crow with delight and shout,
"Oh! You still like butter!"
then crown me with the daisy chain
they've made.

And I shall know
when they are very old
(say one-o-one)
they'll catch the sun
and grow – sunflowers.

Much of my time was spent indoors and I was very aware that many of my links with Nature were secondhand and stirred only mildly by printed images.

Lost Realities

Why do they stir the heart:
images on greeting cards,
glossy adverts, old prints,
faint murmurings upon an inward ear
of long-forgotten music, or
names which start
a trawl of memory, teasing a tear?
Is it because that tender sense of awe
which once made time to stand and stare
now brings small recompense,
less easing of dull pain? Where
the redbreast on the spade's handle?
Freckled poppy fields? Nightingales in rain?
Cool trees in sunshine whispering?
Bright-eyed heifers jostling through a country lane?
Have they gone? Or have we lost the need
to see and feel first-hand?
Old appetites intrude, the questions stay,
as giddily I speed,
eyes glued, ears closed, nerves taut,
upon the motorway.

Even in the early years of my awakening, the gap between the experience of being part of a greater Whole and reflection on that experience felt like belonging to two separate worlds. This was one of my early attempts to grapple with this duality:

The Gravel Pit

Within the heart of the forest, a tangled path away
from lines of stiff, red trunks, rough arrowheads
of branches and long, straight rides
of tired grass, a burst of bud-colour, bird-song,
sky-glory erupts, where once the rhythmic play
of human muscle won from the earth great screes
of gravel; stuff for roads, houses, living;
but now the forsaken mounds sprout wild, strong
growth of broom and bramble. Moths, early bees
and chattering finches soar in a wild garden, giving
the trees a new dimension. Sand martins fly,
deer leap in the sunlight, rabbits bob and flee
from the track-way where brisk breezes race
along the gulleys; creatures of a secret Arcady
amidst the planned, repeated patterns of the Chase.

Here is another example of juggling with this duality:

Old-Fashioned Pathways

He stood in denim, sickle raised,
Nature's warrior, poised to trim
bracken, blackberry, hazel, vine,
dog-rose and thorn in Lovers' Lane.
Since nineteen-thirty-nine barbed wire had torn
The flesh of wanderers there.
But now the bright young folk,
steel edges keened by inner fire,
were hacking at impediment.
"Excuse me," said the bramble,
"before you poke away at roots
that I've put down, where
do you think you'll find that rare
spirit who still would ramble
old-fashioned pathways?"
The others urged the stroke
but still he stood, a statue in the loke.
"You know," he said, "I swear the damn thing spoke!"

And, for children, I wrote this in an attempt to bridge that gap:

If You Are Still

If you are still, quite still, you'll hear
an urgent whisper in your ear:
"Don't move! Don't move! For I am near."

Perhaps it is a butterfly,
creased wings trembling like a sigh:
"Don't move! Don't move! When I pass by."

Or else a tipsy bumble bee,
drunk on honey for her tea:
"Don't move! Don't move! If you seek me."

Fescue grasses whisper low,
telling where the breezes blow:
"Don't move! Don't move! That's where I go."

Maybe a vole beside a brook
splashes from its reedy nook:
"Don't move! Don't move! Just stand and look."

A burst of joyful caroling
babbles from a lark on wing:
"Don't move! Don't move! Hear everything."

If you are careful any day
you'll hear the tiny sounds which say:
"Don't move! Don't move! I'm just a breath away.

When, many years later, I had opened myself to new energies in perception, observation and interpretation, I reworked a poem about swallows that I had previously restricted to two stanzas, each one a haiku. It had been the opening poem of a piecemeal collection of poems I was putting together in self-advertisement.

Now I have added a further haiku to acknowledge that we human beings often lack the trust that informs the passage of migratory birds.

A Triad of Haiku

Swallows

To the hum of Hu-u-u-u-u,
symphony of timeless space,
the swallows flew.

Fledglings also knew
the call of that hallowed place
where new life grew.

Oh! We watched them go,
too weak to admit or face
that….. we also know.

Maybe we're more like hedgehogs!

Prickly Customers

The hedgehog is a prickly cuss
(a little bit like some of us).
Go near, he curls up in a ball
and never gets picked up at all,
although the saucer by the door
tells what he's really looking for:
for milk and love he sorely pines
but still he only sticks up spines.
However, though he can't be hugged,
by alley cats he's seldom mugged.

We walk this planet of ours equipped to serve its needs. Our failure to realize this has impacted upon its beauty and balance. We have created our own gods, our own daemons and our own diversions. Now is a time for restoration – restoration of our inner balance.

Then shall the Outer likewise echo our full humanity and thrive with its own integrity.

Earth Echoes

In the beginning we would seek out stones
or, rather, essence in solid form compressed.
A gargoyle rock at rest
in primal forest grinned amused assent
and, everywhere we went, a spirit stirred
within the stuff of stones. We heard it
in our bones… our bones… our bones.

And with the stones came other forest spells:
a distant bird-song, droning bumble bees
and, at the tips of trees,
a sudden whisper to enhance the hour;
whisperings of a power not seen, murmurs that melt.
And then a chilling Silence fell. We felt it
in our cells… our cells… our cells.

Not only in our bones and cells the bud
of universal loveliness takes hold,
but other blooms unfold.
Deep, deep within, red corpuscles awake.
Instinctively our hands make contact, whence
new energy bursts forth. We sense it
in our blood…our blood…our blood.

Alert now to the prompts of zephyr, deva, elf,
we glory in a wealth of shining days.

Ordinary things amaze
and, reflecting outward form, our bodies sing
source-song of everything. Nerve-endings burn
with holy, healthy fire. We discern it in
our ego-self... our self... our self.

But, still persisting on another plane,
our mental selves negate the things we feel;
brand unseen things, unreal,
insist our laws of logic are the Light.
Our sentient selves must fight each fear anew
as all the sombre spectres queue within
our brain...our brain...our brain.

Our awakened soul took note and underlined
the emptiness of disenchanted doubt;
urged us to carry out
the inspirations of our daily round;
prepare, enrich the ground, and find and sow
seeds for the far wiser world we know of
through our mind... our mind... our mind.

With a light finger-touch, sea changes start,
guiding us to share the beauty and the bliss.
No greater joy than this:
to live the heart-beat, feel the tug of soul,
dance to the rhythm of the Whole, the calling drum
of past and future promise. These come from
the heart... the heart... *the heart.*

On a somewhat lighter note, but still in the same vein, I write here of an intruder into a gathering of our Fish Hoek Poetry Group.

Tale of the Wagtail

Remember, Liz, that moment just before
you led us through a mix of words
which made us long for more
when....

> Little trotty wagtail
> flew through the door
> gazed upon our circle and...
> decided to withdraw?

I think my bones are telling me
when they grow tired of words
that they may still remember
the messages of birds.

Already word-play memory
gets jumbled and grows stale;
but not that briefest flash of wings
and the bobbing wagtail's tale.

For June Dormer, with still a mix of reminiscence and present-time event, I wrote this in January 2008. June also senses the essence of the unseen.

June Blooms in January

Ten years ago, a hemisphere away,
I wrote about June roses picked in winter rain;
and yesterday I saw that glow again.

They were such sudden gifts, I wrote,
more candescent carmine
than their summer selves
because they wear a blush
of unbelonging.
Their glow
from bed of artemisia gray
and white camellias in blue cut-glass
brightened a bitter day.
I did not know
what trick of circumstance
had fooled their genes,
nor could I foresee
the repetition of that chance
Epiphany.

So, when you left two roses in a glass
inside my unlocked door without a word
it made me think how extraordinary
the pleasure that such random gifts ensured...
June blooms in January.

IV

CHILDREN OF TRANSITION

The section following this one contains a selection of poems that describes transformations occurring in the lives of adults, particularly myself, as we fall under the influence of higher frequency energy pulses now reaching our planet.

With children, however, it is different. Many of our children born post-1980 are pre-programmed to function within the limits of this higher frequency energy and exhibit behaviour that may sometimes seem inappropriate for meeting the requirements of old energy systems and institutions. They are children in transition. Hence the newly-named "disorders" like Attention Deficit Disorder (ADD) and Post Traumatic Stress Disorder (PTSD). Drugs like Ritalin, designed to block or dampen down "hyperactive" responses attributed to the release of dopamine to post-synaptic receptors within the brain, are being increasingly prescribed during children's early formative years.

It is as if a fertile imagination, such as that possessed by Mozart, Einstein, or Jung, was an impediment needing medication to reduce its radical impact. The great original creators were never content with "more of the same".

The inner frustration of children forced into the mould of institutions inappropriate for their healthy development – the holistic growth of body, mind and spirit – leads ultimately to social alienation and rebellion.

My first poem in this section pays tribute to the resolve of our Indigo Children who are carrying for us much of the stress that inevitably accompanies rapid changes in perception while the second, "Seaside Friends", cites an instance when the old and the new paradigms are contrasted. The remaining poems are about, and for, my grandchildren who very definitely are Indigo Children.

Indigo Children

Indigo!

Somewhere between the rays of blue and violet
a half-seen colour melts its misty haze
into the bottom arches of a sparkling rainbow
astride False Bay.

Bright-eyed children spot the essence easily
and recognize the theme; for they
were born to see more clearly
what we have only glimpsed in dream
before today.

They're kids who will not yield to grown-up hectoring,
nor confuse the preaching with the deed,
but, holding on through all the lecturing,
set their course for where their heart-beats lead.
Then, from the life-blood that has ceased to flow,
they'll take their leave.

Although they'll ache and grieve,
knowing what they know, they'll also sing…
"No! No!
We've seen the hidden sheen
of Indigo."

This was written for Heidi Svoboda, in Kessingland. Nine years old at the time it was written, she was definitely an Indigo Child.

Seaside Friends

On Summer Sunday afternoons
Melissa, Jane and I
forsake the world behind the dunes
for sand and sea and sky.
We plunge and dive and play about,
stirred by the wind's sharp tang,
and laugh and sing and sigh and shout,
a lively, happy gang.

Beneath a broken groyne today
– half wrecked by last night's storm –
intently watching us at play
there sat the strangest form:
a girl with trailing golden hair;
her skin like pearl; and pale
green limpid eyes. I had to stare
at her curled fish's tail.

But, stranger still, although I cried,
"Quick Jane! Melissa! See?"
My friends stared blankly, said I lied,
And turned away from me.
The little mermaid combed her hair
and smiled a dazzling smile;
then gently asked me if I'd care
to go and swim awhile.

She plunged into the foaming deep
and turned to beckon me.
I stood perplexed, as if in sleep

facing the lonely sea.
I had no tail, no golden hair;
my eyes were not sea-green.
I felt I could not venture where
I'd never, ever been

But then within I heard a strain
of music far away
which called me to the sea again.
I left my friends at play.
How can I tell the sights I saw?
Resplendent coral shrines;
vast treasures of King Neptune's store;
thick-jewelled, deep-set mines,

where hushed, so hushed, the hue and cry,
and soft, so soft, the spell,
I felt I'd never say Goodbye,
I loved it all so well.
The mermaid sighed and took my hand
to lead me to the shore.
"You must go back to your own land."
"Please! Let us swim some more!"

"Already you have stayed too long."
She tossed her golden hair.
"But you can listen for my song
when next we've time to share."
She handed me a deep-sea shell
and dived beneath the foam.
I sought my friends, my tale to tell,
But they had both gone home.

For Kumar at 21 months: Kumar is the firstborn of my daughter, Maria, and Ivan Massyn.

Shell Castles

January;
The crowded beach a carnival of sound;
and grandson, nearly two,
sat in rapt delight upon his granddad's knee,
a spell-bound watcher, listener,
dreaming of gleaming castles
scattered through a world that's yet to be.
He watched his mother powering the gaps
between meek bathers in the tidal pool.
She clambered out and waved, but he
was now engrossed in something he'd enjoy.
Two little Indians, a busy girl and boy,
were dredging from a rock-bound tidal pond
handfuls of shattered abalone
to build a small shell castle on the sand.
Grandson slipped down and joined their play,
holding out a tiny hand
brimful of fragments.
Three smiles, inverted rainbows mirroring the sun,
sanctified his gift. Although their work-rate lessened
and the castle did not grow as fast as planned,
the playmates shed in common cause their differences
of gender, age and race
made manifest in their spontaneous game
with earth and water; they already *know*
deep, deep within the subtle, burning flame
of Indigo.

Another beach episode with Maria and Kumar made me very aware of connection over the generation gap.

Measure for Measure

February high tides and Atlantean waves
had driven screeching gulls from the sea wall
on to the shrunken strip of beach
where craven chicks, waddling within close reach,
arched scrawny throats expectantly
for half-digested tidbits from the sea.
And you, in infant empathy,
set forth to join them.
They, not yet full-fledged,
half-skimmed, half-flew
to fortresses of rock sea-safe from you.

So lazily we strolled
to meet Mama returning from her run,
and counted shining berries in the morning sun.

Then, once more beside our beach-bound rock
while Mama swam, you looked up to behold
an old, old man, now wheelchair-bound,
pushed to the very edge of his sea memories.
You toddled off to stand and stare
as nurse and daughter helped him to his feet
that he might hobble, hesitant and slow
along the board-walk, trusting in their caring.

"Ow!" you said, feeling that walk of pain.

You went on staring, and, in his chair again,
he stared right back, slowly stuck out a hand,
bony, blotched, gnarled, twisted, shaking...

You took it, held it, returned his smile.
Even the fledgling gulls forsook their craking
such was the communion that graced the giving, taking.

Another one for Kumar:

For Kumar on his Third Birthday

Strange as it may seem, I was once three
and received for my birthday a bright, shining trike.
I rode straightaway for the whole world to see
for, having three wheels, it wasn't a bike.

Scooting off on my own was a hair-raising thrill.
It was fun to escape, especially when
I would pedal like mad to the top of the hill
and, with feet held up high, hurtle downhill again.

We lived at the time on a council estate
at the edge of the town with not many cars;
and when I rode out through our garden gate,
I pretended my trike was a rocket to Mars.

Halfway up the hill lived old Granny Fitch.
She was old, she was crinkled and ugly and short.
My sisters both said she was a cranky old witch,
till she caught me one day – and charmed off a wart.

I still can remember what it's like to be you,
to go off all alone and feel you are free.
I recall how tiny it felt to be two
And find it's no different when you become three.

And for Kumar at 4 years and 3 months:

Muesli and Marbles

June and just after Winter Solstice –
you came with Nana, Dadda, to the tranquil flat
fronting Clovelly wetlands.
The door grille yielded with a mighty cl-a-a-a-ang …
you leapt into my arms, more weighty now
than in your babyhood;
my ancient bones barely withstood
this battering – but my heart sang.
Such energy!
The greetings done, you asked for muesli
which you munched while we three oldies drank our tea.
Then you unearthed the marbles
and, craftily,
embroiled me in your game
of scattering;
so much more *fun* than all that nattering!
The missiles reached a dozen hiding places
till end-time came;
and you were so *good,*
dragging all the furniture from where it stood
and peering here – and here – and here –
till every one revealed its hidden self.
The marbles, back upon the shelf,
you ran outside, and, waiting on the grass,
you called out vulgar words like "bum" and "arse"
while you were waiting by the car.
Why do you switch off the shining light you are?

Again for Kumar at 4 years and 8 months:

Tyrannosaurus Rex

Not quite Christmas and you were feeling spent,
not really caring if you came or went.
Comatose from hours in the car,
you thought Clovelly beach a beach too far.
But then you felt the call of sand and sun
promised you such games of fantasy and fun,
you had to heed the murmur of the sea.
For a while you wandered aimlessly,
and then you drew your pictures in the sand,
such detailed scratchings only you could understand.
Sundara, wanting to join in, complained when she
was pushed away; and so you turned to me
to seek support. We found quite soon
we'd taken on new characters – me, an old baboon,
and you, Tyrannosaurus Rex, red in tooth and claw,
though I was eighty-seven and you were only four.
They were just daft games boys play when they're at war.

Sundara, Kumar's baby sister, was born seven months after their father died in a road accident. Before her birth, Maria arranged a welcoming ceremony in Tokai Arboretum.

Gift for Sundara

You were still to be born when your Mama proclaimed
a pre-birthing ritual, beneath ancient trees
in Tokai Arboretum, where you would be named
Sundara, the Beautiful; goddess of these,
and friend of the wounded, the poor and the maimed.

And all who would bless you were requested to bring
a gift from the riches our planet provides
to seal our thanksgiving for Life's everything
and to welcome your coming, whatever betides,
that throughout your life your heart may take wing.

Then your granddad asked Kumar – your older brother –
if he'd like to give you a lock of his hair
to show that he cared for the life of another.
He said "No!" so crossly, you'd think he'd no care
for granddad, Sundara, dead father, or mother

But knowing how way will lead on to way,
his granddad decided to ask him again
and questioned him gently, quite late in the day,
believing that no act of love is in vain,
"Won't you really give just one lock away?"
On that charmed afternoon as we gathered to bless
the way of your coming, when this tale was told
and the grove was awash with love's tenderness,
at this point of telling, with expectations on hold
from the crowd, Kumar's voice exploded "Yes!"

V

Poems of Transition

The Pain of the Body

When I wrote the first draft of the introduction to this section of
Not More of the Same, I initially allocated it to Section IV. Section IV
now features "Children of Transition".

It was only while I was thumbing through a sheaf of poems for a
suitable title that I came across an old draft of the first poem of this
section. It was a poem I had virtually forgotten I had ever written,
even though it was the product of convalescence in a hospital bed
as I recovered from the most intensive bout of physical pain I have
experienced in my lifetime.

It came towards the end of the ten happiest years of my teaching
career as headmaster of a small rural school at Great Hockham, in
Norfolk. My wife, Paddy, and I were living with her mother and
father in a large chalet bungalow we had jointly planned and had
built in the neighbouring village of East Wretham. Situated in the
heart of Thetford Chase, in seven acres of farmland, it is a veritable
Eden. Our two teenage children, Sandra and Derek, were boarding
at Wymondham College some fifteen miles or so to the East.

Everything seemed to be perfectly in place. And yet … and yet
…

The onset of a deep abdominal pain, a post-midnight ambulance
journey to the Norfolk and Norwich hospital and an emergency
three-stage colectomy challenged the perception I had at that time
of the lineaments of happiness.

Emerging from the first of the three surgical interventions
I experienced, while still in the operating theatre, what has
been defined in recent concessions to the validity of subjective
perceptions, a near-death experience.

There is no sequence of chronological time or separation of
physical space in the mind's processing of psychic information
that higher frequency energies provide. In the aftermath of severe
physical trauma I saw simultaneously from a vantage point above
the lights of the theatre the surgeon and nurses surrounding my
supine body, the figures of my family gathered around my recovery
bed and, when those images faded, a brilliant light at the end of a

long, dark tunnel through which I hurtled at an incredible speed.

It was then I heard the cadence of a voice that has been a reminder and a reference point ever since:

"You think that you have suffered. Yet there are others in this very same ward who have journeyed further into the dark than you can ever imagine."

"I know. I know," I mumbled.

"To end things now, or to return and share the suffering: the choice is yours."

The voice faded. A roaring ensued, whether internally or externally I could not tell. And then the pain returned. I could feel where the surgeon's knife had sliced the skin of my stomach and dared not allow my hand to explore the site of his incision.

I allowed one eye to slide open. I was back in my bed in intensive care and not another soul was in sight.

'Drip Feed' was the first of a series of poems that I wrote in hospital. It came from the deepest springs of my being and heralded my own transformation.

Drip Feed

Life-giving fluid, drip by drip
probing the body tissues,
dissolving the years' accretions,
cleansing, feeding, vitalizing
and teasing back the light of knowing
into pain-racked eyes.
And there – there in the void – surprising
intimations of what is Being;
cosmic issues that span the ages;
a strange, detached serenity
that recognizes primal innocence,
and re-asserts the physical
validity of the flesh;
an unveiled seeing of the alien actions
we inflict upon our lives,
our twisted bodies, wrecked nerves,
disordered minds. Again, again, again;
drip... drip... drip...
sustaining, without our knowing,
our true selves.
Drip...

This poem was how I recorded the agony I felt, three days after the initial operation, when my surgeon was in theatre and no further painkillers could be added to my intravenous drip until he was available to give the say-so.

The Pain of the Body

Never once does it relent,
the sometimes sharp, now mind-blurring,
now merely nagging reminder of the wounded flesh.
There is no other world but that of pain –
and in the background the voices,
the cheerful cogitations of life's vain
shadows that mask reality.
Read the papers, and yet once again
read the papers, listen to the news
to hide away from truth. Life hurts.
Living hurts. Being me is too demanding.
But wait. Pain still insists upon its voice
and will not be ignored. The papers
are laid aside. The voices fall quiet.
The mind is snatched back
to its prime concern. In agony
the darkness closes in.
And there, there in the extremity
of bodily endurance, the thread snaps.
I yield. The self steps down at last,
and listens in the quiet to that which still is
beyond the ends of pain.
The kingdom of heaven is within you.
Perhaps that's how we die, yielding the self,
yet knowing that what we have yielded
is only the shadow and even pain and death are
but paths to Truth.

This one was written for Maria as she was emerging from the early grief of losing her partner.

On Setting Out for Haga-Haga

On Africa's Atlantic coast a Scarborough water-hole
and all those bright young people
feeding back to you the essence of your giving:
sun, and spruit, and surf, and sea,
abundant jewels of the wrenching joy of living;
strong, enfolding arms, clear eyes, cool company
of true familiars set in children's laughter....
And yet ... and yet ...
Beyond the rapture still another goal,
an inner yearning, a need that lingers after
even friendship's ecstasy
– a cry of soul.

Deep within, you know each little barque
of flesh and bone must ever sail anew
for unknown shores, breasting the looming dark,
the icy calm, the grieving rain.
The wind that strains its sail
propels towards a Whole.
How can you sing star-music
unless you cross the bar
that separates you from the self you are?

Your Haga-Haga, when you enter in,
will verify the One beneath your skin.

I return now to a reflection upon the numinous experiences that had accompanied the beginning of the transformation process.

The Key

Black velvet, laced
with a cross-stitch of stars:
moon-rise beyond the trees,
leaves silver-traced
and lazy longings poured into a limpid night
while still the heart sleeps.
By day the sun, bright with dawn promise,
shines through prison bars
on millions busy with their daily tasks
in bustling, clamorous marketplaces –
sleepwalking, maybe, so inscrutable the faces,
so fixed the masks.

Nothing is changed: night follows day,
the old earth tracks its ancient pathway,
the moments flow;
but suddenly, all things are turned about:
now is forever, and below, above;
beauty erupts and heaven's within, without,
all fused together in the birth of Love.

And this one is virtually a plagiarism of an old pre-war song that I sang at Open Mike night on my 88th birthday at Hugh Hodge's "Off The Wall" poetry session here in Cape Town.

Dreaming…

Dreaming …
Just idly dreaming …
Dreaming and scheming
of how my life could be …
I could be a baker,
poet, music-maker,
but I've only been a Quaker
living quietly.

Oh, may we trust our Watcher,
the Watcher who has got yer,
that's if the Watcher's got yer
following your own star.
No need to be a Big Name.
Like millions just the same,
it's time to be the one you truly are.

And this, I think, was the first real poem I ever wrote after coming out of hospital back in 1964. Some years later it received a Crabbe Memorial Award in the UK.

The Yellow Hammer

I heard her first in the heart's darkness,
the singer who, like the stuttering yellow-hammer,
sang her own song. So all birds sing
when Love's impulse suddenly vibrates
upon the inner core, the God of everything.
And then I longed to make my heart a cage
in which to keep the yellow bird, so to release
her mystic harmony at will. But Heaven's rage
was awful… awful… making all songs cease,
spilling a chilling silence everywhere,
stilling the little bird. And so,
reluctantly, I set her free,
not dreaming what new dawns she'd bring to me.

And this one recalls a meeting with Maria's mother after she returned
from Austria when Maria was six years old.

The Ghost Without a Voice

"It must be years!"
Our eyes met over the double-creams
but what my ear hears
is a luke-warm greeting.
We're strangers now,
the memories bitter-sweet and fleeting.
Who are you?
Did you once invite me to the inner room,
opening windows direct upon your dreams?
Laugh carelessly? Whisper? Sigh? Ring true?
How is it, then, you speak in alien tones
of matters and of vistas strange and new?
And who am I?
I recall the hours
when I would wait upon your every word, cry
rapt approval, sense your latent powers.
"Three, at least," I say, and sip my tea.
The ghost is voiceless whom you seek in me.

Casting around for guidance through the despair and emptiness of being once again on my own, I sought spiritual clarity by renewing my links with Quakers. Among them I met Jack Richards, at that time joint warden of Beccles Friends Meeting House. He was a man of great integrity who lived his understanding more, I think, than anyone I had met before. This poem, "Exile", arose from the conversations and activities we shared:

Exile

It's all right for you.
You've tramped the Inward Country,
laughed at its trackless heights,
found foothold on far ridges,
fallen, and crawled from deep crevasses;
stamped your own path.

Me?
I need bridges,
highways, passes;
evidence of firm ground,
before I leap.
You say I'll learn
to take by leaving,
hold by letting go.
How can I tell you're not deceiving?
I need to *know*.

Two of the main guiding insights of Quakers are 1. that the Light is
present in everything and 2. that God, the Principle that underlies All,
is to be found in the Silence. It is this wordless omnipotent, omnipresent,
omniscient source that the following poem seeks to express:

Where the Sap Flows

One truth remains
distilled
by the long, listening years:
words are not silence-filled,
nor do they bridge the inside-outside fracture.
The Babel Towers we build
are grotesque follies
designed to ease our fears.
Although a lifetime's wordplay feigns
a kind of knowing,
it is when Silence reigns
we hear sap flowing.

For the sap of autonomous and authentic growth to flow it is more important to listen than to speak. "The Listener" is a poem I shared in a Quaker Workshop on Creative Listening soon after I took up residence in Cape Town in 2001.

The Listener

I drip
poems from an open wound,
nightingale songs which derive their sweetness
from the raw edge of pain
expecting, perhaps, each bloodied word
to take from me the enduring ache
of loneliness; hoping yet again
that, mingling my words with yours
to seal our love, I'll make
the great journey across the void.
But you had heard
in the first word
my lonely cry and, from your equal hurt,
reached out to comfort. All along
my voice has sought your ear;
your ear, my song.

Each one of us is always, in all ways, on the way home.

Homecoming

Not for one moment in more than eighty years
have I unloosed the silken ties of soul.
Perhaps in childhood
when monstrous fears
urged peer conformity
I'd fake compliance, swallow lies
but even then I knew – I always knew –
the goal.
And, though it seemed my silence sanctioned perfidy,
I'd not give voice to the malicious cries.

And in my teens? Ah! That was the time for tricks!
How hard it was to swim against the tide!
I tried – oh, how I tried –
to learn to swear, to drink, to lay the chicks
but never once outreached my inner guide.
And still loud, outside voices urged me on,
leading to the familiar wedding aisle;
only for me to stumble when, first passion gone,
I had to flee the emptiness awhile.

Lonely, I sought some further echoing heart;
tearful, I felt the planet's piercing pain;
angry, I watched the center fall apart;
yet, still I knew… or thought I knew…
until that voice which ruled my heart
called me to task, "You know you cry.
But still you will not spread your wings – and fly."

And then… and then, the graveyard beckoning…
two tiny embryonic buds unfurled;

not really wings in my crass reckoning
but just enough to lift me from the world.
"Live what you know!" I urged my ancient cells.
"Be what you are!" I coaxed the living flame,
then hurtled through a million earthly hells
until – I heard the forests call my name,
saw a setting sun give rainbows birth,
knew how birds, bees, babies, wordless came to know,
found that my home was where the zephyrs blow;
and I became the richest man on earth.

The final poem in this section (perhaps still too cerebral) identifies the moment when participation in a Transformation Journey first crept into my consciousness. The Journey still continues.

Chair in the Corner

How could they know?
…………………..
Had I not sat brooding there
while the years scuffed the armchair
and the urge to speak?
Upon the stove the good wife's saucepan bubbled,
creating patterns for the pipe-shaped fiends
that granddad curled into the telly's shriek.
Across the room in rhythmic rage
the busy needles purled,
where grandma grimaced at the weekly page
of gentle grumbling from the kids at school,
while I sat silent in the corner. Only a fool
would think our hearts were troubled.
……………………..
How could they know
my foolishness had come of age?

VI

POEMS OF PROTEST

I Can't Hurt Anymore

The ambiguity of the title of the first poem in this section is deliberate; it being meant as both a statement of extreme, and an indication of the end of inner pain. Most of the poems in this section belong to a period of my life when anger sparked both thought and action. It was the heyday of the Campaign for Nuclear Disarmament (CND), the mass marches to Aldermaston and to sundry nuclear weapon bases in East Anglia, as well as huge rallies in Hyde Park. Local Hiroshima Day activities also took place on August 6th each year to refresh our memories of the carnage caused when Hiroshima and Nagasaki were nuked in 1945.

"I Can't Hurt Anymore" presents a sequence of low points in my life when external events tested the extremity of my endurance. It was to be many years before I was enabled to see that I, too, was part of the shadow and that love has to be unconditional if it is not to be manipulative.

It is followed by a number of poems that were my way of, at the time, externalizing my anger until … until … I don't know **when** it actually happened, but I know that it did. "I Can't Hurt Anymore" became "I Don't Hurt Anymore".

I Can't Hurt Anymore

There was a day when I was ten
and the window broke.
I wilted at the look
my father threw at me.
No questions; just a glare.
I fled up the back stair-way
and cried and cried. Life's so unfair.

But now, when fingers point, I just ignore.
You see, I can't hurt anymore.

In teenage years I had a dog,
name – and nature – Pal.
Better than any gal
I loved that hell-hound.
Went missing. Dragged a paw
and metal trap to our backdoor.
I couldn't weep, I was too sore.

And now, when creatures writhe in oil or gore,
I freeze. I can't hurt anymore.

Your first love's one you don't forget;
and mine was a wench
during the war, of French
Huguenot stock. Her
smile lit up red hair. She
sweet-talked promises from me
then said one day, *"Alors! Meet mon mari!"*

That's why I no longer count the score
of liars. I can't hurt anymore.

In middle age I tried the path again
– surrendering the heart.
I thought it was the start
of something special,
the birth of our princess.
When she was nearly seven, I guess,
She was plucked two continents away, no less.

So now when families split through hate or war,
I sigh. I can't hurt anymore.

Still later, in this rush of frantic years
with not a thing at rest,
Peace at its very best
has overtaken me.
Old age shows how I've grown,
through all the shocks to which the flesh is prone,
and no longer fear the vast Alone.

At last the heart-wound does not feel so raw;
life's lesson learned, I don't hurt anymore.

The frustration, anger and heartache of that period of my life found its first release in projection upon outward events and people. I "took up arms against a sea of troubles", joined in the Campaign for Nuclear Disarmament, and went on marches, vigils and demonstrations. I have chosen only a few poems to convey the direction of the growth occurring under the surface of protest. This short verse conveys a mix of arrogance in my pacifist condemnation of modern warfare and the burgeoning altruism of my concern for the nature of the planet we bequeath to future generations of children. It was written in the early 1990s when the Iron Lady sent Britain's armed forces to recapture the Falkland (Galapagos) Islands.

Rock-a-bye, Little One

Rock-a-bye, Little One,
listen to me!
Our bombers are bombing
and you shall be free.
No need for nightmares
or screams in the night,
to keep you quite safe
we will put out the light.

This was the time when Michael Heseltine, Cabinet Minister in Margaret Thatcher's government, descended by helicopter upon the Cruise Missile base at Molesworth in Cambridgeshire and gave orders for the Peace Chapel the Peaceniks were building there to be demolished.

Rainbow Images

"We had a good thing going there," she said,
pinched cheeks, sad eyes, blonde head,
a terror-haunted child;
drop-out, of course, wild wastrel.
"I didn't want to leave."
You could tell
the young man loved his goat.
"Over the hill they came," he cried,
leading it on. "About midnight,
with their barbed wire. They fenced us in."
As ancient chalklands sighed,
a woman's bitter laugh
and swift, astonished stare
met the reporter's question:
"What do you say to those
who claim your camp defiles
their landscape?" Nose
to tail, the lorries gnawed the miles.
The lady at the pub,
wild in another way,
showed that she bore no love
for Monet, or for rainbows (nor knew
how lovingly the campers preened their caravans).
One lonely soul by candle flame
prayed in the half-built chapel
while others sang of peace
until the soldiers came.

And later still, the hero, battle-dressed,
descended, god-like from the Molesworth skies
to boast how he had set about the quest
to blow this candle out.

*An evening broadcast on BBC television by Bishop Leonard, Bishop of
London, claimed that the war against Argentina was a just war, and
thus repeated the age-long collaboration of Church and State to present
a united front against dissent. My chagrin was such that I wrote a letter
to the Bishop.*

My Dear Lord Bishop,

When you spoke last night
about the virtue of the British cause
and why, despite the cost, such Holy Wars
must be pursued to teach a moral right,
another candle lost its feeble light
to utter darkness; the task was yours
to point a way to open doors,
to strengthen souls that waver in the fight.
Instead, you praised the pardonable might
of national righteousness, upheld the laws
of legal force, failed to indict
the us-and-them presumptions of false pride.
How could you deny your Christ inside?

My late-life odyssey has mellowed the angst of those earlier protests,
but the feeling is still there, as is evident in the poem that follows. Our
Fish Hoek Poetry Group was asked to present a poem about rejoicing.
My immediate reaction was to recall the Iron Lady's words from the
steps of Downing Street in response to criticism about the sinking of the
Belgrano in the South Atlantic.

The Silence of My Rejoicing

Let the sound of my rejoicing
make way for Silence.
If I seek to ease the pain
of innocents in the wake of mindless violence
by voicing the merit of an eternal glory
I compact the anguish of the slain,
deny their story.

Oh, I know the joys of resurrection
from my own defeats
but the way was mine. I cannot tell
the path by which your life completes.
To urge connection with an everlasting Dharma,
I assert a prejudice that could well
delay your karma.

Ever since the Iron Lady
bade us all rejoice
at the Belgrano's sinking in the southern seas
I have hesitated before giving voice
to such causes for jubilation;
pondering how paeons such as these
affect creation.

So let rejoicing now be muted by
its concomitant,

the voiceless shock of preternatural death
sprung suddenly upon a babe or infant
mass-executed by some thoughtless would-be hero
packaging a bomb to blast a child's new breath
to Option Zero.

No! I cannot rejoice, not anymore,
in the collateral vulgarities of War.

VII

Heart Limericks

For a little more than a year now, I have been reading my poetry at Hugh Hodge's "Off The Wall" Open Mike Sessions in Observatory. It provides a wonderful opportunity for poetry lovers and writers to bring their own or their favourite poets' work into a public arena, as well as the chance to listen regularly to published South African writers. Occasionally a spot of music is tossed in as well.

It is always a live creative experience, memorable because of the quality of the listening and Hugh's affirmation of those who participate. I never fail to depart from its evening sessions inspired and invigorated.

However, not surprisingly, some of the tensions of our post-Apartheid society find ready expression, and sometimes the anger is palpable, drowning the beauty of the words.

Mea Culpa! You've just skipped through a section containing my own poems of protest, which indicate my readiness to use poetry as a therapeutic tool when dealing with anger.

So I figured I'd try to write a series of limericks to lighten things up a little. The issue that comes to the fore in almost all is the severance of what Carl Jung calls *the animus and anima*, or the masculine and feminine elements of our psyches. Over centuries of the *animus* being in the ascendancy, the divide has gradually widened and the social and cultural structures that arose – church and state institutions, social roles, family and work hierarchies – are nearing the end of their relevance to the task for which they came into being. Hence the turmoil in human interactions all over the planet. This section contains some of these poems, ones of a lighter vein.

Bunkered

When you wake up feeling half dead,
finding it hard to get out of bed,
if your heart never feels
what the moment reveals
it's because you are stuck in your head.

Lesson of Life

It has taken this cosmic corpuscle
nearly ninety years hustle and bustle
to remember its heart
(though it knew from the start)
is more than a bloody big muscle.

Body Language

I could not feel the strength of my bones
or hear the shrieks of my body's hormones
till I'd fled down the years
from the blood, sweat and tears
and the allure of erogenous zones.

Animus and Anima 1

He seemed like a regular guy
standing there in charge of the braai
but at soft pillow talk
he was a bit of a dork.
It takes a strong woman to cry.

Animus and Anima 2

It's hard for a man to conceive
that ever since Adam blamed Eve
they've been embroiled in a fight.
Can't we both get it right
before Life's vital spark takes its leave?

Anima and Animus 3

Her original steady said, "Madam,
you'd not use your brains if you had 'em
All this crass Women's Lib
from a flipping spare rib?" –
But his scorn brought come-uppance to Adam.

"Enough is enough!" muttered Eve.
"I don't care what you believe.
Just you nibble this apple
and I'll pray in your chapel
– for a while – but you'll never conceive."

Anima and Animus 4

I grew up with angry young women, irate
at the yoke of their second-class fate,
in a world built to scale
by the astute alpha male
drunk with his desire to mate.
So it's such a delight to relate
that now I'm a chaste eighty-eight
the same angry young ladies
don't think I'm from Hades
and give me a hug without hate.

Descartes

You'll remember that fellow, Descartes
was the one who took thinking apart
when he thundered out, "Damn!
I think so I am."
And broke every feminine heart.

Old Misery Guts

You could tell at a glance that his face meant
that she was on hormone replacement
and, because of the static,
kept her pills in the attic
and his Viagras were locked in the basement.

Advice from an Oldie

When you find you're kind of back-tracking,
and the old zest for living is lacking,
you're still not bereft
of the time that is left,
so get off your butt and get cracking!

The Way to an Early Grave

Don't tell me you haven't yet found
your reason for being around.
It's always been purging
and surging and urging
– the you that you drove underground.

Mea Culpa

I didn't know what fun it could be
to feel frothy and friendly and fulsome and free
till I turned things around
and suddenly found
I could laugh at this sad little, mad little… ME.

And, finally, it would seem appropriate to let the tribute to Hugh Hodge and the "Off The Wall" motley, be expressed in limerick form:

Off The Wall

From Cape Town, the UK, even Texas
new voices contribute a nexus
and, once in a while,
elicit a smile
that explodes in the group solar plexus.

VIII

Trail-Blazing Journeys

I've heard it described as "Jumping off the edge of the cliff", "Sailing into the Unknown", "Being Re-born" – and all sorts of other metaphors (or are they euphemisms?) for changing one's life direction. Often it amounts to no more than altering the external scenery (shifting the deck chairs on the Titanic?). But sometimes, although increasingly more so, as the nature of the energy of evolution filters into human consciousness, the shift occurs in body, mind and spirit, an holistic metamorphosis into a new experience of being.

I begin this section of *Not More of the Same* with the most recent poem to have been teased forth by my muse, "The Way of the Trail Blazer". Chronologically it should, perhaps, appear as the very last item of the whole anthology, but in the new way of being there is no linear sequence, no "ought" or "should"; no "if" or "but", no "when" or "meanwhile", only **here, yes, now.**

All creative acts are acts of surrender to an *imperative not yet known by experience*; only in that way can it *become* experience.

All the rest of the poems in the section, although they portray the same dynamics of creation at the time of their writing, have led to this point of being. The joyous delight of the "Trail-Blazer" comes at the moment of realization that nothing, *no-thing,* can be judged to be "wrong".

"…when you give your All to your Life-Task", the poem concludes, "then you will see the splendour, and the vast reach of it."

So here we go, blazing the trails of new experience:

The Way of the Trail-Blazer

Listen!
Do you not hear that constant hum
seeking your rapt attention?
– a thrumming that contains a heritage
of connection, faint cosmic cadences
of far-off star-burst
syncopated to the forgotten drum-beat
of a universal theme?

In the beginning was the birth of possibility,
Glimmers of perfection in the arts of Being,
Living, Thinking, Doing,
Playing, Hearing, Seeing;
releasing glimpses of a Lake of Beauty
and a scourging by the Forge of Truth.

"No," you sigh, "I do not hear your music."

Awake from dream!
Your fear's lost cry
prolongs the heart/mind split
and masks reality.
But when you give your All
to your Life-Task,
then you will see
the splendour, and the vast reach of it.

This poem "arrived" when I was suddenly struck by paralysis of my lower limbs in the Spring of 2004.

A chiropractor diagnosed a misalignment in the skeletal structure of my lower spine and insisted the power to heal lay within myself. When, after three weeks, I could still only move with the help of a crutch and could scarcely lift a shopping basket, I allowed myself to consider and accept the prospect of the remainder of my life permanently incapacitated.

With acceptance, my physical balance gradually began to improve and eventually I was able to function in a body that was more flexible and mobile than it had been for years.

Sailing Into The Unknown

Almost unceasing since October dawned blood-red
above the Helderberg,
wild South-Easters have snatched and slobbered
sand-smeared shards of foam along the crested brows
of False Bay's springtide surges
and I've felt an inner storm
scouring the hidden depths which lurk beneath
this little barque of flesh and bone
and, in desperation, clung to threads
of knowing what I've always known:
We mirror what we find without, within.

– until we find it is the other way about.

Pitching and tossing in the squalls of pain,
star-path obscured, breasting a looming dark,
my legs a broken rudder, only my soul
somehow aware the wind that strains my sail,
the icy calm, the grieving rain
are elements to guide me to the Whole.

How can we reach the stars
unless we cross the bar
which separates us from the selves we are?
Before my birth my sails were given me;
before I traded words, I heard the wind.

My affliction and recovery brought into my consciousness other
"inexplicable", "miraculous" events and encounters that led to new
ways of thinking and being. This was one of them: a recollection of the
time when Maria had returned to the UK to study for her A-levels
when she was seventeen years old.

Suburban Miracle

From the waiting years you had emerged
eager, fervent for identity.
Some veiled need for dynasty had urged
you to track down the country of your birth
– and me.

Ipswich station is not exactly Paradise,
but somehow it set my antennae aglow.
To meet you once more, that would suffice;
and, more than that, we were to take in
a West-End Show.

That's why I stood, far from the vale of tears,
lost in a reverie of patterns never drawn,
waiting, waiting, as I had throughout the years,
teasing out the labyrinth since you
were born.

The connection for London was running late,
and two young lovers wrapped in new-found bliss,
strolled the platform arm-in-arm. I visualized their state
as they replayed the past I
reminisced.

At the platform's end they turned, came back
and, as they passed, she slipped his side,
threw her arms around me by the track

and kissed me on the lips. I laughed
… I cried.
I'd never held much store for miracles as such –
all I could say was, "Thank you. Thank you so much!"

Miracles? Inevitably this return to my consciousness of the powers of
primary perception *led me into contact with people and experiences*
that were not limited by the constraints of the logical, rational mind.
That shift had started among the pine trees of Thetford Chase and
eventually brought me to South Africa and Fish Hoek. It was here early
in 2006 that with Astrid and two of her friends, I participated in The
Transformation Game, a new-age invention that involved dice, cards
depicting either inward growth or impediment and a processing board.
Superstition? It didn't ring false.

The New Board Game

I hadn't played with Angel cards before,
at least, not seriously.
Though within past dream I sometimes heard and saw
ethereal guides who wisely counseled me;
so I was not completely unprepared
for insights from the hidden depths we shared,
nor yet surprised when one of us declared
her current game, for her, had been profound.

A bold quartet it was, who sat around
that drop-leaf table in my Fish Hoek flat,
awaiting briefings to activate, astound,
or put to question old perceptions that
tied each one of us to our defunct daemon,
– the ugly duckling that forswears the swan.
With set intent, we each one looked upon
the turning cards that probed the heart's deep core
and teased us to process our mistakes of yore;
for these were not stiff fingers damning sin,
but gentle nudges opening a door
to ancient wisdom already held within.
So telling, they brought forth a primal scream
from one entrapped in man's unyielding scheme

to be top-dog; sprung tears for the brave dream
of Angels' acumen,
Archetypes
and wild, wise women.

Let's see how that compares with perceptions back at the beginning of the Dark Night of the Soul. This was written back in the 1960s after a solitary walk through the darkness of pine trees in Thetford Chase on the night of a new moon.

The Night Forest

Darkly, they stand, the reaching limbs of pine;
darker, darker tonight than when their red trunks
glowed on a moon-full evening. Silently they climb
skywards, losing their form, their singleness, chunks
of vague shadow masking the sharp, fine
needle-prick of stars. Silently I trudge the woodland way,
its atmosphere unfelt, the Now-Time
banished to a faded yesterday.
I cannot perceive the tree-ness of the trees, and they shun me.
Did they ever breathe soul whispers in the wind?
or burst new life from chattering cones in Spring?
or tell the world the secret that we shared?
Though in my inner dark remembered echoes ring,
The singer's gone who taught my heart to sing.

*The most challenging of all transformational journeys was undoubtedly
my uprooting from the UK and relocation in Cape Town at the age of
81. Before setting out I tried to capture in words the myriad emotions
that accompanied that time of not knowing the outcome.*

Disentanglement

When shadowed dark obscures tree-shape,
when sap-flow ceases
and roots are least alive,
it's Winter, and transplanting time.
Why, then, now my winter self
seeks out new earth
in which to thrive,
this pain
of disentanglement?

I sit among marked boxes
and the frozen clutter
of past years:
old poems, postcards, photographs
and tax returns.
Adrift in tears,
I relive episodes
first screened in technicolour,
but now replayed in sepia.

As from this settled past I tear my roots
I find they are encased
in soil which nurtured me
through storms of yesteryear.
I know they'll strike again
in new-turned earth,
but there is loss, as well as gain, in change.
The pangs of budburst we once shared
come back to haunt this last farewell to you…
and you… and you…

IX

Time Travelling

The few poems that found their way into this Section of *Not More of the Same* owe their inclusion to varying forms of self-reflection. It is very clear to me that I am not always tapping into the full consciousness of my autonomous self. Sometimes my thought is circumscribed by the insights and feelings of the immediate now. Sometimes I am lured into the past, sometimes into the future and sometimes the nature of the thought brings its own gift.

However, the very nature of poetry demands that it be the product of such realities being considered reflectively and shaped by the self-in-the-making. If I were converting events to poetry at the time of their happening, I would not be paying full attention to the experience of them.

A couple of years ago a poet friend of mine sent me the following extract from preparatory notes for Breyten Breytenbach's poem, "The Grave of the Unknown Poet":

> *Poets aren't incarcerated or tortured for their poetry – at least, not very often: the powers that be, have been, shall be, prefer to lobotomise their poetry, and it is a more refined form of torture. Poets aren't a nation. Poets aren't a class ... Poets form no ideological group. We are made up of ... the attempt to make ... love poetry, hate poetry, mind poetry, finger poetry, poetry of resistance, poetry of commitment, poetry of the belly-crawl, empty poetry, poetry of poetry; we try to make that from which we are made. And sometimes a little more. Maybe the poet has something of the soldier, the political prisoner, the god – who knows, even the torturer. But (s)he is a human with a drumskin perforated by sounds and sights and feelings. Leaking words. The poet is just a human without a skin ... That which links us all is exactly the unknown. We are all covered by the absence of skin ... In every poet there is the poet unknown.*

It is because I regard the act of writing poetry as a form of time travelling, and Breyten Breytenbach echoes this, that I have given the first poem in this section the title, "Back In My Skin".

Back In My Skin

Here I am, back in my skin,
yet
for an instant I touched eternity.
(The waves told me, and the sun's sheen
glacial white along the line of their breaking;
birthing whales piping a dark and ancient meaning,
and lovers everywhere forgetting separate selves)
all linked with me in one brief, dazzling moment
of recall.

I try to pare that ageless alphabet
in hope of making
a sound which, like the wind's keening,
startles the slumbering cells
into a rare and icy sentience
of Being.

But you, seeing
only the wrinkled husk of my spirit's casing,
hearing its awesome words at second hand,
cannot join me in the soul's chasing
to the far reaches of the One and Everything;
the outer Eden, and the world within,
– unless, of course, you dare yourself take wing.

Then, maybe together, we will smile
at scent of lavender in the Pleiades.
Meanwhile, I am content to be
here in my skin.

*"In These Strange Days" was written before I made the long external
journey to the Southern Hemisphere, not only to reconnect with
Maria, but also to be a part of the dynamic that was seeking to replace
the recent ravages of Apartheid. Although my first impressions of a
burgeoning South Africa were of a nascent reawakening, vestiges of the
old also began to make themselves felt almost to the point of déjà vu, as
if to suggest that these 'strange days' were global rather than nationwide,
maybe even cosmic.*

In These Strange Days

In these strange days
a pre-dawn dream breaks through
the bounds of sleep
to breathe a half-heard whisper urgently:
this dream, this dream's for you.
Be still and hear
your ancient voice.
Be true
to its old harmony.
The hurt, the pain,
the nightmare of a million memories
are dreaming you.

Dreams spell a need for change,
and deep, deep, deep,
you know what they are calling for,
you know the tale they tell,
the phantom messengers
of these strange days.

This one I wrote for the 2008 issue of "Scenic South in Focus", but I guess it wasn't sufficiently embedded in the corporate economic mores to be included therein.

Let Us Sing the Songs of Tomorrow

Let us sing the songs of tomorrow
and, giving full voice, let us say,
"We are done with the bondage of sorrow
and are full with the gifts of today."

Let us sing the songs of the mountains,
the thunder of rivers in spate,
the murmur of whirlpools and fountains,
and the lilt of our own little spruit.

Let us sing the songs of the ocean,
chant the rhythms of storm and of calm,
feel the throb of our heart-cells in motion
relating to tempest and balm.

Let us sing the songs of the creatures
who share this fair planet of ours,
take note of their exquisite features,
their habits, their nature, their powers.

Let us sing the songs of creation
that appear now with increasing pace,
heedless of culture, or nation,
or species, or gender, or race.

Let us sing the songs of the spirit
that is free from the fictions of fear,
accepting all things on their merit,
and holding impediments dear.

Let us sing the songs of tomorrow
and, while miracle music holds sway
in Fish Hoek*, let's beg, buy or borrow
the shoes that dance to them – today.

*Please substitute any location of your choosing.

X

SHARED AUTONOMIES

If You Would Make Music

The most exciting discovery to have come from this odyssey of increasing awareness has been the intimation that it is the outcome of a journey shared. The initial euphoria that accompanies the breakthrough into autonomous selfhood is readily abrogated by the ego, determined, as ever, to assert its separation and superiority.

Recognition and acceptance of one's own autonomy is incomplete unless it is accompanied by the recognition and acceptance of the autonomy of others, including that of single representatives of other species. Yes! **And** the mugger and hijacker; the rapist and murderer.

"Whoa! That's hard!" you exclaim; and that's for sure.

Whoever thought that shifting the mind-sets of millennia only needed a little huffing and puffing?

So I begin this section with the poem "If You Would Make Music", a poem originally written for co-creator Astrid Larsen and an affirmation of her and your contribution to the cosmic symphony, even if everyone else is complaining that you're singing off-key.

And suppose, just for a moment, you had agreed to take on the role that enables another to experience fully all the dimensions of forgiveness. Would that make your oppressor a guardian angel?

So the theme of "Shared Autonomies" is developed. Its concluding poem, "Star Children", boldly asserts: WE ARE ALL STAR CHILDREN.

Take, hold and cherish your own autonomous self.

If You Would Make Music

If you would make music
be still and listen
to strains of your own lost memories
replaying agonies of star-birth,
symphonies of sun,
euphonies of earth,
supersonic echoes of The One.

Underneath our epoch's repetitions,
beyond the aeons' soulless screams of fear,
you'll hear an old, persistent heartbeat
faintly throbbing on your inward ear;
drumming, strumming in a wordless language
of a Light that is forever near.

Listen well and spread your music's glory,
open up your heart and set it free;
for every one of us must tell our sacred story
to join the song that sings the world to be.

This is a cameo to remind me of the unexpectedness and pure joy of experiencing shared autonomy in the most unlikely places and with strangers who, through some gift of primal perception, become known familiars.

Unspoken Messages

Still young in heart, although I'm creaking old,
and sitting on a handy bench to rest,
I do not feel myself thus set apart
but watch the world go by, my day on hold.
Three Xhosa girls, still in their later teens,
dance past, and one, encased in light,
stops at a bright display of future dreams,
then slowly turns, catches my eye, and *knows.*

Her hand comes up, brown fingers fluttering
in greeting and, for a moment, my young heart can sing.

For, not only babes-in-arms, these children of the dawn
but teenage seekers too, eyes bright, equipped to frown or smile,
daring to challenge, question, air their "No's"
and, heart-centred, to walk the extra mile.

No need to tell me these were "Indigoes".

And, here, a reflection on the stuff of dreams:

The Ghosts of 4 am

4 am
and still a mad South-Easter
lashes the surf below.
A creaking window-frame grinds teeth at ghosts unseen
as if it, too, has been where I have been;
into a place where only madmen go.

Was it when I dreamed that place, they came,
the broken spirits that disturbed my sleep,
who, once upon a time, would weave and wed and weep
in fairy tale? I could not name them,
but I recall the human claim they made
by dint of twisted limb, unfocused eye,
imaged in the limping of the lame
and in the whispered longing of their sigh.

What wounds are burdensome enough to sap our human powers?
What makes us see such suffering souls as *them*?
Whose forms are these, whose scars, but ours,
which manifest themselves at 4 am?

And, here, a covenant with the autonomous beings of tomorrow:

Sacraments of Soul

I pledge you both, star children,
all my remaining years,
that you may tap life's energy,
its wisdom, laughter, tears;
and know that naught can harm you,
or pluck you from this bond.
It rests upon past synergies
and stretches to Beyond.

(True, when I went to shave this morning
and found my razor blade awry,
I thought – my wits so slowly dawning –
How come? – Oh, yes! Kumar passed by!)

And when Sundara sits and looks
and looks – and looks – and smiles,
it tells me more than all my books
to ease the absent hours and stretching miles
that Time and Space plant in the way
between her path and mine;
for she and I have shared the ray
which daily makes Creation shine.

Already both of you exude
Aquarian frequencies,
the New-Age, New-Heart, New-Thought energies
that can't contain themselves but must explode
with passion.
This, I vow:
you both received such wondrous gifts before your birth.

And now
it is for you to recognize
your special task,
to mend, revitalize,
and heal this grieving earth.
If you need guidance – ask!

There is sharing not only with those of family, or whom we know, but also with seeming antagonists.

Creative Anger

A summer day along the deserted boardwalk
from St. James set me off day-dreaming
of the Rainbow Nation I had come to seek.
A young man, who'd pushed from Muizenberg
his brand new bike, gleaming, spotless, sleek,
scarce glanced at me as I said, "Hi!"
Nor did he speak.

Oh well, I thought, *it just takes time,*
and what's ten years after Apartheid's gall?
Instant change is arbitrary. All
things are meant to be. And who am I
to judge, in any case – a three-year resident?

The call of rolling surf and cloudless sky
recaptured me, and I dreamed on.
Then, all at once, the sound of running feet
clattered upon my reverie. The passer-by
had leaned his bike against the sea-wall
and raced back to me, screwdriver held high.
"Give me your money, or I'll use this!" His mugger's cry.

But there was something … something … in his stance
That did not ring true. Maybe that sideways glance?
– And I was angry, disturbed dream angry …

"How dare you!" I stormed.
"How dare you go round threatening old folk like me?"
His jaw dropped and, as I warmed to natural ire,
I said, "If you had had the grace to ask,

I might have found as much as you would find
if you spilled blood." He shuffled. My guts caught fire.
"What's your name?" I ventured, feeling for my loose cash
and thinking: *Maybe… maybe… this is rash,*
and here's how it all ends.

"Nigel," he said, and dropped his weaponed hand.
"Mine's Lewis. Friends?"
He took the clutch of coins and, transferring them,
held up his empty left in Afro-style exchange.

Strange, this pugnacity of men before they see
the common threads of their humanity.
and even then I had to have my say.
"Don't ever, ever, try that trick again!"

He smiled, "*Siyabonga*, Lewis." Went on his way.

Often others willingly take upon themselves some of our burden and ease our pain for a while.

Mirth

A laugh bursts,
filling my emptiness
with splinters of reassurance,
relief.
The puerile antic of a natural clown, frantic
with supra-human woe
is therapeutic. The false belief
that only he suffers,
struts in mistaken mastery,
is vulnerable, absurd,
grotesque, frail;
only he fails,
gives me a moment's brief
forgetting of the pale
Watcher, the one whose silent mirth
applauds my act.

And another fragment for LeRoy Cowie, with thanks for his fun-making.

Fragment

When I shuffle words into a shaft of meaning
I escape awhile the raw wind's keening
and, when you offer me a listening ear,
we both are liberated from old bonds of fear.
Yet something more I would still ask of you:
when this joy of mutual trust is through,
will you strive to hear, continuing
the haunting music other Muses sing?
For always there are echoes true and just
from myriad voices before they turn to dust.

Another poem for Astrid on her 51st birthday.

Star Child

I weave this labyrinth of Love
with threads unseen
save when a hint of gold
illumines what has been
and draws upon the shadows
of the Dreaming
for a truth that's never old.

WE ARE ALL STAR CHILDREN.

And when that cosmic gleam
falls upon a single shooting star
hurtling through the dark
to seed another galaxy
with possibility, Creation's vital spark
fires everything – the heavens, the earth,
the unformed matrix of new being ...
               ...you and me

XI

A Spiral of Altered Repetitions

She

The title of this section is one of those enigmatic aphorisms that requires a bit of effort on the part of the reader. Did your inner critic whisper in your ear, "How can they be repetitions if they are altered?" And then, "Don't repetitions always return to the starting place? How, then, can there be a spiral?"

It is precisely these paradoxes that the poems of this section set out to address.

"She", the first poem of the section, was written back in the 1990s when the frayed edges of gender roles began to impinge upon my awakening unconscious. Ostensibly, the *she* being addressed was my muse and where better to discover *her* true lineaments than in the blood-and-flesh manifestations of the feminine in my own life?

Already at that stage of my life I had walked out on my first marriage and been walked-out-on in a second long-term relationship. What were such dislocations all about?

In "She", I trace the inner journeys of the *anima and animus* in my own psyche and hint at how subtle changes come about at various stages in the life cycle. So the repetitive learning process continues, but in altered form, as it proceeds from a point of greater awareness.

The ascending spiral constantly leads towards unconditional love and the rest of the poems in this section reflect other stop-go points on this journey. At such critical points, we liberate higher-vibrating energies into the functioning of our neural pathways and open up greater possibilities.

Equally, we cannot rotate or ascend on a spiral of altered repetitions until we have made the last step our own; a ready expression of our hearts, as well as an understanding in our minds.

The poem "Only" indicates what a slow and laborious process this may be; very often the task of a lifetime.

And always, all ways, the impediment lies in our fear "to go the whole hog"; to act from the similitude of our own divinity.

She

She came long ago, I remember
in the owl hours before the dawn,
slipping into waking dreams
like an instant sigh.
More child than woman,
her flesh was firm, her embraces sure,
her power invisible.
The knife, with which she peeled off
youthful parody,
sought febrile blood.
She knew I had to feel
raw pain.
Her gift lay in the wounding.

And I remember, when the sun set fire
to frith and fount and fell,
she cooled my eager blood
with hint of weeping.
Dripping stored sadness,
her form renewed itself in me.
Fissures and fragments fused.
The myrrh of other seasons
choked my hubris,
assuaged my pain.
She reached to re-create my
creature.
Her cure lay in the reaching.

After the healing, I remember,
she was ever by my side
arranging a rendezvous
with her companions.
Her shrewd compassion
led me to the self-deluded,

the frauds, frail, famished
and forsaken, the disappeared.
She prodded me
to share their loss,
and give tongue to their
bleeding.
Her love lay with the losing.

Now we are alone, just she and I,
in the bat hours before the dark,
lured by ultrasonic sounds
which haunt the night.
Still she rouses me,
still pulls together sound and sense,
rewarding me with pleasure.
Her final pricks are patient
half-reminders
of her presence.
She knows I'll soon lay down
the "I".
Her gift comes with the leaving.

Often I become conscious of the cultural and gender bias of another age, in the work of such giants as William Shakespeare. Here is the anima response to Jacques's speech in As You Like It.

The Seven Ages of Women

The world is not a stage,
nor are its women merely actresses.
Life lives them with perennial duress.
First in infancy, when stirred to tenderness
by the transfigured frog beside her pram.
Then with schoolgirl tears for each defenceless lamb.
At seventeen she falls in love and, less demure,
a fever in her blood, she feels quite sure
that she can care for two or even three.
It's then she starts to lose identity
and, drained as Mother/Wife, exhausted, chafing, sore,
she wonders if things matter any more.
Then, once again, she braves the brooding dark,
determined in Man's world to light a spark,
as slick executive with every hair in place
and not a trace of pity on her face.
In that grey world she toils for dignity,
anxious to leave her mark for all to see,
but feels shut out from honeyed halls of power,
and soon she finds her clock has passed its hour.
Now menopausal, lost, hostess to tears,
she mourns the faded beauty of the years.
Last task of all as, like her hapless mate,
trembling and frail, in sad and sorry state,
but practiced in the arts of Life's short day,
she does not die, but gives herself away.

And, if I may make so bold, an added dimension to the biblical family prayer:

A Prayer for the Age of Aquarius

Our Mother.

> who shapes all earthly forms,
> may all your pain be blessed,
> your gift be honoured,
> your compassion thrive
> in human hearts, as in the world of Nature.
> Enable us to share in your self-giving,
> and forgive us our unknowing,
> as we forgive those who share the dark with us;
> for yours is the witness,
> the spirit and the love
> to birth this Age and Ages still to come.

Amen.

Of course that is what poetry does, it creates a new spiral from old repetitions. Here is an attempt to give form to that process.

Birth of a Poem

Words sing

They daub their coloured crotchets on the wings of sleep
– whether the crimson spurt
of a last heartbeat,
a midnight blue of sorrow
from a last hurt,
black minims from the soul's dark realm of night,
or the bright drumbeat of a glimpsed tomorrow
– all the sonic colours intertwine
to shape a rainbow symphony
in which I cannot tell your song from mine.

And then I wake and try to write
this weave of tonal warp and weft,
this moment's needful rendering
of songs sounds sing.

If from that shrinking pool of love,
the stuff of soul,
these words were born,
they will transcribe the tears of this torn
world, and sing them whole.

Without this forward movement into further areas of possibility, life would be static and sterile. "Dream", however, reminds us that often, in our arrogance, we colour our aspirations with the colours of our self-indulgences.

Dream

We dreamed ambrosial dreams:
huge fantasies of never-ending pleasure;
of torrid hours, the jaded sense to thrill;
of ecstasy, designed to fill
time without measure.
We dreamed ambrosial dreams,
and woke to human ill.

We dreamed Promethean dreams:
bright visions of a vast technology
spawning new tools to hasten revolution,
to change the life of Man and institution,
and forge democracy.
We dreamed Promethean dreams,
and woke to mass pollution.

We dreamed Arcadian dreams:
sweet idylls of demure rusticity;
of sanctuaries beyond the city's hum,
rich heartlands where howls of greed are dumb,
and all's simplicity.
We dreamed Arcadian dreams,
and woke to squalid slum.

We dreamed Elysian dreams:
of heavens above the ken of mortal man;
of misty views beyond the pearly gates
of Paradise, where angels stand and wait

to shape God's plan.
We dreamed Elysian dreams,
and woke to stiff-necked hate.

I slept without dream's mask,
and woke to this day's task.

And we are – or, at any rate, I am – usually slow in challenging the imperatives that others place upon us. "Only ..." traces some of these procrastinations:

Only ...

I think that I was barely three
when my mother said to me,
"You must join in or you'll be lonely."
Only ...
"Come on. That's not the way to be!"

At just nineteen I went to War.
"These are your enemies," they swore.
"For your country, fight and die."
Only I ...
"Be strong; ignore the misery and gore!"

At forty and with a family,
I fell beneath the spell of She
and, of course, she had a plan.
Only I can ...
"Here's what you must do for me!"

Set in my ways at sixty-eight,
I heard the preacher sternly state,
"Believe, or you'll end up in Hell!"
Only I can tell ...
"All right. Then you must meet your Fate."

At eighty and still going strong,
I found new ways to get along
though I was prone to spit and cry.
Only I can tell my ...
But what if I had read it wrong?

The doctor says, "You're ninety-plus.
You must put your trust in us.
Take these pills." *What? Dim my glory?*
Only I can tell my story,
and if I need to curse at me – I'll cuss!

So I await this body's final rest,
confident it's passed the cosmic test,
only … only …
why, for others, do we think that we know best?

This poem resulted from an exercise in a creative writing group in Fish Hoek that examined the same words from opposite time perceptions: a concrete example of "altered repetitions".

Intimations – A Dream Palindrome

Last night I dreamed I was intuitive.
I could not grasp it at first.
Understanding filtered through only as the dream took shape.
I was alone wading through the marsh, a strangely sombre, familiar wasteland.
The air was heavy with moisture, clammy, evocative of ghosts.
Striking through the thin fabric of a summer shirt, coldness chilled to the bone.
My heart quit beating and I gasped for breath.
In the gloom of the marshland it danced; an eerie, flickering light.
A Jack-o'-lantern, I told myself; it leads you to destruction.
I stared.
The iridescence danced, bobbed, weaved along the path.
A radiance lit up the tips of my bare toes.
I could feel a warmth, subtle, reassuring, full of promise, flooding my body cells.
"I am the image of things to be."

"I am the image of things to be."
I could feel a warmth, subtle, reassuring, full of promise, flooding my body cells.
A radiance lit up the tips of my bare toes.
The iridescence danced, bobbed, weaved along the path.
I stared.
A Jack-o'-lantern, I told myself, it leads you to destruction.
In the gloom of the marshland it danced; an eerie, flickering light.
My heart quit beating and I gasped for breath.
Striking through the thin fabric of a summer shirt, coldness chilled to the bone.

The air was heavy with moisture, clammy, evocative of ghosts.
I was alone wading through the marsh, a strangely sombre, familiar wasteland.
Understanding filtered through only as the dream took shape.
I could not grasp it at first.
Last night I dreamed I was intuitive.

Here is another one reflecting on the art of poetry. It gives weight to the spaces and silences, as much as to the words. Again, a case of "altered repetition".

Silences Between the Words

A poet knows
wherein the secret lies.
Not in the rhyme,
the rhythm
nor the repetition;
but in the emptiness
that waits upon the word;
recognition
of a moment shared in Time.

Brimful of images is that telling moment:
the frozen posture of a damaged child;
a bereaved mother's ceaseless, silent tears;
the stretchered, bleeding soldier;
a dolphin's piping cry that haunts the night
and stirs the frightened creatures of the wild;
anguished flutterings of a migrant bird
confused in flight
by man's intrusions with the sights and sounds of War.

And we,
stunned by words and bomb-blasts from the TV screen,
do not hear the sobbing
in the silences between.

At 89, I have developed a friendship with a wonderful co-creator, Astrid Larsen, who has hugely enriched the dimensions of these later years. It is grounded in mutual trust and respect for each other's Soul Journey, and is free of the more blatant demands of desire and ego-gratification. We freely give to each other and freely receive.

"Hold My Hand" is also written for Astrid, not in supplication, but in acknowledgment of the existential aloneness that is our common lot. The way we have supported and honoured each other has far surpassed any previous experience of bliss in either of our lives.

Hold My Hand

Hold my hand…
I do not crave the clamour of the crowds;
I'd sooner feel affection of the few,
unspoken nearness,
linked little fingers,
see the shine of looks that spanned
the vast Alone, to let me grow.
Oh …!
Hold my hand!

Hold my hand…
I do not seek the fever heat of fire;
I'd rather find a center calm and still,
a quiet core,
a place of peace,
where I may rest upon a golden strand
of real belonging; be and know.
So …!
Hold my hand!

Hold my hand…
I do not need the everlasting arms,
unless they have that subtle skill of touch,

throb of pulse-beat,
heat of heart-blood,
that magnify those moments quite unplanned
when fearless feelings flow.
Oh …!

Hold my hand!

Many of my life encounters have been with single mothers and their daughters. This was written in 2007 for Anita Lotz, another co-creator, and her daughter Beverley.

Mothers and Daughters

Greetings from a buried Animus
upon a day when Love's destructive dark
all but obscures old images of Being.
The tiny spark of self-hood,
from which you grew,
flickers in disbelief
at the strange contours of a New Self
you are now seeing.
Can you believe you're You?
A single Mum, a re-awakened child,
an emerging Valkyrie,
sporting in the fierce, wild
surf of a forgotten sea?
Live life again, then,
in a Rainbow Africa,
and learn the language of the stars.
This is no time for repetition:
the red tide, the False Bay smog,
the rainbow fragment
of a sundog near the horizon
are not the lineaments of dream,
nor are the phantoms of the mist
quite what they seem.
Beyond the frisson of uncertain fear,
your super-self arises adventurous and near.

XII

Poems of Continuing Connection

Requiem

If this anthology of verse has not conveyed a sense of interconnectedness with past and future, with far and near, with inner and outer, with nature and technology and each of us one with another, the title of the final section offers one last chance. These are poems taken from experiences that point, I think, to Continuing Connections.

We all catch glimpses of unity in diverse moments of time, in the appearance of differing things in space and in varying intensities of feeling within ourselves.

The task of the poet is to clothe such glimpses with words, in the hope that they may spring open the doors of perception.

It is, therefore, no accident that "Requiem" automatically selects itself as the opening poem of this section.

You are familiar by now with the outline of the life-story that brought me to South Africa at the age of 81, to reconnect with my youngest daughter, Maria.

A little more than three years after my arrival her partner, Ivan, died in a road accident leaving her with a two-year-old son and an unborn daughter.

"Requiem" was wrenched from that constellation of typical South African events, as an attempt on my part to address the perennial flight of the human spirit from acceptance of the inevitability of physical death.

Sufficient is it to say that Ivan, post-July-2004, became for me and, I believe, for others who fully registered the shock an even greater reality than when he was with us in life.

The introductory note for each of the other poems will point to the reason for their inclusion in this epilogue and suggest that our quest for understanding and the unfolding of the unconscious are differing facets of the same continuum.

For Ivan Massyn, died 06.07.2004.

Requiem

How do you write a poem to untimely death,
the inspirational breath wrought numb,
fine senses dumb,
deep feelings dulled against all future sorrow?
Write now!
Now, while the torn heart
cannot contain itself in this frail
envelope of flesh;
while blood and tears
still intermingle in the emptiness
before the wreckage and the mess
are sanitized by music, poetry, wreaths of fresh flowers
and cards of mourning edged in black.

It was *your* death which perched upon *your* shoulder
along that lonesome journey to tomorrow.
Not mine. Not ours. Thank you, Ivan,
reminding us and putting us on track
for our own journeying. You will be back
to laugh and cry, have fun, be wild,
through your infant son and unborn child.
With them you will release these chains of fear
to reveal a precious pearl in every tear.

Back in 2003, Astrid and I were invited to attend the opening of a new art studio in Lakeside. This poem encapsulates that experience.

Faces of Africa

New, and yet old, that lowly Lakeside dwelling,
rescued from the mouldering hand of Time
to house free, soaring images of soul,
sighed, shuddered, all but cast its shell.
Who were these chattering invaders?
Surely not the ghosts of Bloomsbury,
fifties Broadway, or Montmartre's existential hell?

Where were the faces of authentic Africa?

Beyond the ebb and flow of human concourse
in a tiny crowded room, bold colours glowed
which overleapt the throng;
so vibrant, visceral, so manifestly strong,
they called us back, when space allowed us pause
to stand before three portraits
        – all Eureka-charged.

Three faces of a toiling, troubled Africa.

Our cells aroused, we sensed some hidden theme
of suffering as sacrament to human woe.
The paintings vividly made plain
how body contour contends its spirit dream;
how light of eye and gnarl of skin
mirror a doubt, a quest, a weariness within;
and how all co-creators feel another's pain.

Magic, the moment that we both could share
before the image of that final head.
"Worn – like a rock-face – but durable," you said
commending all our toil-torn faces everywhere.

This was a poem that was made into a video by BBC's Look East Television in 1997 for National Poetry Day in the UK. It was read over the air by Roger McGough.

Covehithe

My contours fall away,
breached with the tumbling cliff
by searching tongues of tide.
For millennia they defied the crash
of rumbling storm, the lash of spray
but now they yield their form
to unknown dredgings of the dark sea.
My spinneys rot.

You would not see, beach-comber,
how my old trees die,
their scrawny arms outstretched
in prayer. Too late you would abjure
your pickings, too late declare
that you have heard the murmur
of the sea.

No ants crawl here on my sere grass,
no birds sing; even the gulls' cries
fall mute. Do they know that everything's
in flux? The gray sea laps
at ridge and root and wreck.
My pathways peter out.
My buttresses collapse.
My contours fall away.

Perceptions change with age, becoming more focused on essentials.
While acknowledging the blurring of outward images, this poem points
to an emerging inner wisdom.

Now I Am Old

Now I am old,
and cannot see as once I saw:
blue dart of damsel wings above the sedge,
bright rainbow flush within a fleck of dew,
a thrush's earthen cup in hawthorn hedge
nor hear the snipe dip low towards the mere,
the drone of hoverflies, the splash of vole;
for other shapes and other sounds draw near.

Fine details fade.
I only know the whole
and hear,
from far beyond the teeming world,
a song of soul.

A song
that's sung in all of life's epiphanies
by nymphs of forest, meadow, marsh and sea
that, furthermore, translates the mystery
of struggle, sickness, sadness, pain.

And, though I see but faintly
past realities
now I am old,
the music on the inward ear is plain.

On impulse, on National Poetry Day 2006 here in South Africa, I phoned in to Cape Talk radio with the following stanza when listeners were invited to do so.

for it is here

for it is here

under the crumpled bark

of our experience –

we pirouette Life's dance:

here, in the dark

of root and trunk and branch

sap flows

truths persevere;

a new form grows.

Maybe this is the last gesture of the ego: over the past year or so I have endeavoured to update my will, bring some order to my finances and state my wishes for the form of my funeral arrangements. Maybe there is something a little kooky in dwelling upon such things. I hope Maria and Astrid, between them, may find the spot in Tokai Arboretum where I would wish my ashes to be spilled.

A Valediction

Take, thou, these flakes of ash
and let them spill
neither as remainder,
nor reminder, of only these past years;
but rather as guides to fill
this living moment with paeans of silent praise
salted with tears.

Praise for rebirth.
Praise for the power of death
to interrupt and change
eons of pattern and repetition.
Praise for new breath
to probe once more Life's mystery,
reclaim its vision.

The mystery of roots
that grow a green, so multi-hued
in mix of trembling leaves,
curled moss and weathered stone,
they breathe out balance, beauty and similitude;
a mystery that brings the All
into the Alone..

The All of deeper selves
who beckon from afar,

but linger in this ambience of trees.
An All that seeks to tell,
I Am, Thou Art, We Are!
Go from this residue of ash
and ... fare thee well!

One Monday morning in February 2008, I awoke with the sense that
I had completed my work on Not More of the Same, *but I still had a*
feeling of disquiet. As I lay still, an urgent impulse intruded: "You can't
end on a note of loss and grief even though such was not your intention
when you wrote "Valediction". You must give ear to the "Yellow-
Hammer", the first "real" poem you ever wrote.

 I went through into the lounge where Astrid was breakfasting and
told her of my intimation. While she was washing up, I retrieved a copy
of "The Yellow-Hammer", considered its possibilities in reverse form and
then drafted, with a little juggling of syntax, the following in about ten
minutes. It has been given another title:

Breckland Dawn Revisited

Not dreaming what new dreams she'd bring to me,
reluctantly I set her free.
Shock stilled the little bird,
spilling a chilling silence everywhere;
for I had made my heart a cage
in which to keep her, so to release
her mystic harmony at will. But heaven's rage
was awful … awful … It made all birdsong cease,
for birds *must* sing when Love's impulse vibrates
upon their innermost core, the God of everything,
to awaken hedgerow, copse and brackened heath,
blending voices, as each sings her own song;
dawn-singers, like the stuttering yellow-hammer.
I heard her first in the heart's darkness.

Postscript: yet one more affirmation for co-creator Astrid Larsen.

Unconditional Love

To you –
   who are the quintessence, and yet the bane
   of my today,
   the warmth of sunshine and the cool of rain
   that come my way,
   the sacred pillar and the urge profane
   that interplay,
   the mirror of my inner flux of joy and pain,
   to you, I say:

   I could not love you in the way I do
   were you but a mirror image and that reflection true.
   Through the clash of difference I have come to view
   The secret of our being
   And ... I love you.

Acknowledgements

I thought I could substitute a new energy form of gratitude to all who played their part in enabling me to reach this omega point of being in my present incarnation. But that would mean providing the names of everyone who lives on in my memory or participated in my life.

So, may I first offer my recognition and appreciation to those members of particular groups that have spiritually nourished me at different levels of time and need: The Quakers; The Poets; The Authors of Insightful New Books that have Pointed a New Way; Children; The Physically and Psychologically Wounded; Powerful Women who have Graced My Life; and You, My Readers and Listeners, all of whom are valued Co-Creators of a rapidly unfolding New Life.

I also find the progress of this manuscript into the public domain has brought many very special people into my life whom I would acknowledge by name. For many of them I have written poems, some of which appear in the section 'Poems For People' in the book, but there are others whose gifts have been so germane to its appearance that I shall now expose their love to the public eye.

I affirm and acknowledge:

My daughter, Maria Shearer, and my friend, Astrid Larsen, for liberating the anima in my own make-up.

Hugh Hodge, Editor of 'New Contrast', and convener of the Monday ight 'Off The Wall' poetry gig in Observatory for his open heart.

Anita Lotze for her unfailing encouragement and appreciation of words put together in a different language from that of her upbringing.

Paul Mason and Silke Heiss for their readiness to drive me to Observatory.

Kechil Kirkham and Caroline Blackburn and all the enthusiasts of 'Off The Wall' for their recognition and affirmation.

And in the practical processes of publication, Arthur Attwell and Silma Parker of Electric Book Works, who have been ever solicitous of an old man's shortcomings.

So diverse and indefinable are the unseen threads of connection.

Lewis Watling
Fish Hoek. August 2008

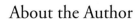

About the Author

Lewis Watling is an 88-year old teacher, mentor and poet, having taught at junior, senior, special needs and adult level schools in Britain, Canada and South Africa. At the age of 81 he uprooted from the tired earth of the UK to join Maria, his youngest daughter, in Cape Town, and renew contact with the vibrant energy that he had first experienced as a British airman serving with the Commonwealth Air Training Scheme from 1941 to 1945. A number of his poems have received prestigious awards and were broadcast in Britain.

He declares that exposure to African energy has opened up channels of consciousness that had lain dormant for most of the previous eighty years.

He now lives, writes and has his being in Fish Hoek, and is a regular at Hugh Hodge's "Off the Wall" poetry gigs in Observatory.